Canadian Wildflowers

MARY FERGUSON/RICHARD M. SAUNDERS

VAN NOSTRAND REINHOLD LTD., TORONTO
NEW YORK, CINCINNATI, LONDON, MELBOURNE

Published simultaneously in the United States by
Van Nostrand Reinhold Company, New York.

Printed in Canada by Herzig Somerville Limited
Bound in Canada by The Bryant Press

DESIGN: ALLAN FLEMING

United States Edition
ISBN 0 442 29850 1
Library of Congress Catalogue Number
76-23670

Canadian Edition
ISBN 0 442 29859 5
Library of Congress Catalogue Number 76-23671

76 77 78 79 80 81 82 7 6 5 4 3 2 1

Contents

Introduction

Across the continent of North America, in Canada and the U.S.A., there are many kinds of habitat. Different wildflowers thrive in each one. Some are unique to one area: others extend from east to west, or from north to south. Interesting differences in the same species may be found in different localities. Out of the thousands of species which grow here, some common ones and some rare ones are shown to remind us of those we might look for in Spring, Summer or Fall.

The purpose of this book is to show the beauty of some of these wildflowers. Since only a very few of thousands of species may be presented, we believe we have chosen some of the lovliest. A common heritage of our two nations, they are one of our important natural resources, adding greatly to the beauty by the wayside beyond the concrete and steel of cities and highways. Our hope is that, knowing even a few of our wildflowers by name and by sight, people will appreciate them in their natural setting and leave them there. If they are not destroyed, they will continue to bloom in our countries for generations to come.

Wildflowers are individuals with distinctive characteristics, just as people are. Each species lives in the home it prefers, and blooms in its own time. Each has evolved by adaptation the way in which it is pollinated and produces seed, and how that seed will be dispersed. Some plants are useful; some only ornamental. Some are edible; others are poisonous. Some are natives, only to North America; others grow on all the continents of the northern hemisphere.

The note with each picture describes these individualities and tells how and why each was named in Latin. The Latin name is very useful and worth knowing. It indicates the family to which each species belongs, and usually, some interesting characteristic. It is a universal name. Common names, even in English, are different in different localities for the same species.

Edible and poisonous plants are identified, but few edible ones should be collected for food except in an emergency. Identification for food must be exact, for some poisonous plants are easily mistaken for edible ones. This is not a botanical guide, but the notes are as accurate as possible. Scientific names are often changed, and it is not our purpose to explain these changes.

Most wild plants do not grow in sufficient numbers to make harvesting worthwhile or wise, lest the plant be destroyed. We wish to encourage the conservation, not the destruction of our heritage of wildflowers. Digging up wild plants for gardens is usually destructive, except where they are being destroyed to make way for highways and buildings. If you want to have a wild garden, collect the seeds. Seeds will be more likely to adapt to a less favorable habitat, while a blooming plant will not survive for long.

All the pictures were taken on 35mm positive film. Most have been taken under existing light; only a few were taken by flash. Almost all have been taken in habitat, as many pictures show. Each photographer has tried to take the best possible picture of the finest example of each species, with a keen eye for its beauty and fragility. What you see may be the choice of many attempts, year after year. Many years of learning, of trial and error, and hours of patient waiting have gone into these results. Most of the photographers are amateurs, in the true sense of that word, who try to capture on film the flowers they love. They took most of these pictures long before the book was conceived and without publication in mind, just for the joy of it.

Though so many photographers are involved, I believe all used 35mm reflex cameras. The condition of the light and the angle of it were chosen to suit the subject wherever possible. Clarity and simplicity are two obvious qualities in these pictures. Backgrounds are often shaded, or blurred by selective focus. Backlighting is used to create effect and a suggestion of three dimensions. For those interested, careful study of these pictures will suggest the methods used.

This book is divided into habitats with their kinds of flowers. Only four were chosen though many other possible divisions exist across the land. Consequently, some species grow well in more than one habitat. In the notes the most likely locations are given. 'Wildflowers live in the woods, but die in your hands' is a plea to preserve them. Many have disappeared from their former haunts due to destruction by man. We pick them, spray them with poison, cut down the sheltering woods and tear up the ground where they dwell. Each year there are fewer to enchant our eyes and gladden our hearts. 'Take only pictures, leave only footprints' is written on a National Park sign. If you love the wildflowers, you may enjoy their beauty for years by taking them only with your camera.

Marshes, bogs and other wet places

No natural resource is more extensive or more precious than water in the northern half of this continent. Indeed, in this regard Canada is one of the best-endowed regions of the world. Flying over vast areas of this land one can see a pattern of interlacing water and land so intricate that frequently the observer cannot tell which is more extensive, the water or the land. Water and wet places are to be found almost everywhere in the country; even on the high, dry prairies there are sloughs.

For well over two centuries after European discovery the waterways, rivers and lakes provided the basic travel and transport system of the continent. Today's international shipping lane along the St. Lawrence River and the Great Lakes is a reminder of those past days. In recent years, with the increasing pressure upon natural resources, the importance of the great network of wetlands as an invaluable natural reservoir of fresh water has become evident. These vital areas are also assuming an ever-growing significance to satisfy the mounting demand for recreation and relief from the tensions of urban life. Every summer cottager and camper, every bird watcher, hunter and fisherman knows about the attractions of water and wet places. Every naturalist who seeks for wildflowers should know about them too.

To many a canoeist or boatman upon our summer lakes and streams the discovery that he is floating in the midst of a flower garden on the water comes as a great surprise. With paddle raised or motor stilled he drifts into some quiet cove, along some secret channel, finding himself all of a sudden with bird song overhead and all around a fascinating array of fragrant white blooms. Thus unannounced he has come abruptly into the midst of one of nature's wonders, a water lily haven. In northern waters, coming around some spruce-edged point, the paddler can find himself surrounded with golden or red-tinted lilies, the striking yellow pond lily or bullhead lily of the northland. Further to the south, on some late summer's day the shores may be set aflame by those tall, vermilion-flowered plants, the cardinal flowers. Cardinal flowers are red lobelias and not far away the visitor might well discover the equally impressive rich blooms of the great blue lobelia, the cardinal flower's close relation. A walk along a wet shore or perhaps beside a tumbling waterfall in many parts of Canada could be rewarded by the sight of the misty blue beauty of yet another lobelia, Kalm's lobelia.

Many a fisherman, while sitting patiently on some stream bank waiting for a bite, has had his attention caught by a myriad of dancing orange blooms not far away. In the fall these blossoms will produce wonderfully explosive green pods, which give this plant the intriguing name of touch-me-not. Homeward bound, the same fisherman may muse upon both the floral beauty and the fishing possibilities suggested by yet another water garden, the long shoreline beds of pickerel weed.

Paddling along the trail of the water lily the canoe's progress may seem barred by green walls of cattails and bulrushes rising high above. But an extra push brings the paddler out into a quiet pool, flower-studded and surrounded by green. This is a fresh water marsh, one of those hidden worlds which will yield up its secrets only to the eager and respectful traveller. Here is the haunt of the wild duck, of the red-winged blackbird, the painted turtle, the muskrat and countless other creatures. Here also is a realm of flowering plants as distinctive as the animals and birds that keep them company. Water lilies may be here in astounding quantities or in discreet little companies. In some far off corner an enticing mat of gold turns out to be a cove filled with bladderwort. The yellow-horned flowers float on the water and give no indication that under the surface there is a whole lacy network of fine leaves all fitted out with a system of little traps, perfect for catching mosquito larvae, water fleas and other such delicacies which are preferred fare for this carnivorous plant.

Closer to shore, perhaps in the muddy edge, appear the showy white blooms of the arrowhead, while in the wet meadow alongside the marsh splashes of blue indicate the presence of wild iris or blue flag. Later in the season the marsh verge may glow with the deep pink of swamp milkweed or the smoky purple of Joe-pye-weed. And in eastern Canada there may be explosions of vivid purple where the purple loosestrife, that newcomer from Europe, has taken possession of many a marsh.

Not all marshes have navigable water; many have no noticeable water at all. Some may be seen from high banks, others approached by foot along the edge. However the flower seeker makes their acquaintance, he will be sure to find a reward.

Closely related, yet distinct from the open country freshwater marsh, is the woodland swamp. Swampy wet areas often develop through the gradual growing over of a marsh, and during that process there will have been a steady change in plant and animal life. Such wet woodlands have their own communities of living things. Red-winged blackbirds and teal give way to birds like wood thrushes and wood ducks, muskrats to squirrels and marsh plants to swamp plants. No complete shift may take place and much overlapping may exist along the borders; but there will nonetheless be a real change of emphasis.

One of the more striking of the swamp dwellers is the wild calla or water arum, which holds up its immaculate white spathes in shallow pools and along the muddy borders of the swamps. This sturdy little plant is a close relative of that other inhabitant of the wet woods, the Jack-in-the-pulpit. In the fall, Jack's red berries will glow in the dark woods like jewels, but those of another swamp plant more resemble sheets of flame. So spectacular can the autumn glory of the winterberry or smooth holly be that anyone who has seen it in some suitable place between Newfoundland and Minnesota will never forget the sight. In two parts of Canada, southern Ontario and British Columbia, the first evidence of spring will often be found in the swamps. In Ontario the gaily mottled hoods of the skunk cabbage, encircled with snow and rising from spring-fed mud, in late February or early March offers the welcome sight of the first flower of spring. In British Columbia a quite distinct plant of the same family, the yellow skunk cabbage, raises brilliant yellow spathes in the dark swamps at the same time. Thus, from earliest spring to snowfall the swamps are worthy of our attention.

Of all the wet places none is more interesting, and probably less appreciated, than the bog. Distinctively northern in character—indeed, tens of thousands of square miles of northern Canada are covered with intricate networks of spruce bogs known as muskeg—bogs are scattered over much of southern Canada and the northern United States as well. This distribution is closely related to the pattern of former glaciation for wherever the glaciers came, leaving behind their hills of deposits, altering and blocking natural drainage, bogs have been formed. Since many of our bogs have a glacial history, to explore them is to step into the past. The cool, moist habitat of bogs favours northern plants and so we recognize at once, by the presence of black and white spruce, northern cedar and tamarack, that this is the vegetation of the northland. These southern bogs are islands of the north. If, therefore, the miles of northern muskeg are inaccessible to most people, the closely related scattered bogs of the south are available to all who have a mind to explore.

Bogs may be fully grown over or may have at their heart a pool or pond, the last remnant of the open water with which most of them began. All are likely to grow over in time, so we find them in various stages of development. Compared to marshes and swamps they are very acid, so that only certain plants are able to live there, making up a quite distinctive plant community.

Not all the members of the bog community are always represented but one is almost invariably present, the sphagnum moss. This may be clustered in clumps or spread out in thick, wide-ranging carpets through which the explorer must plough knee-deep, learning from experience that this is one of the most absorbent materials in the world, holding water like a sponge. In most bogs that have a pond at the centre the explorer will eventually come to an open mat of low-growing plants. Stepping onto this mat he will soon become aware that the 'land' is shaking beneath him: he is on a quaking bog. Then he will remember that the cover of the bog is really a mat of plants growing out over water and he will be careful how closely he approaches to the edge of open water where the mat may not be thick enough to bear him. Pausing to look around he will find that he is encompassed by rings of green receding into the distance, evidence of various bordering plants at different levels, and he will feel the quiet hush of this private place. He is perfectly safe in this secret world as long as he respects its notably special nature.

Out on the open bog the explorer may discover that he is walking through stiff-leaved little shrubs hanging with pale pink globules of beauty; it is the bog rosemary. Close at hand he may see what looks like a myriad of roseate shooting stars. These graceful flowers will produce those wonderful red fruits, the cranberries, which have graced so many Thanksgiving dinner tables since colonial days. Both these plants may be found as far north as Labrador and Greenland, the cranberry as far west as Alaska and the Pacific coast. Rising stiffly above a nest of green and red-tinged hollow leaves are the purple helmets of the pitcher plant, unerring traps for unwary insects which provide this carnivorous plant with its food. In a higher part of the bog can be found the arching white-belled branches of the leatherleaf, white-flowered Labrador tea, or possibly the pink-cupped blooms of the sheep laurel, all three members of the bog-loving heath family like the bog rosemary and the cranberry. In June and early July the golden yellow lady's slipper appears and the truly regal cream and rose blooms of the Queen's lady's slipper. If the bog has a little stream flowing from it, the explorer may find a drift of rosy-white plants which on closer examination will prove to be the fringed, lacy loveliness of the bog bean. Later in the season he could easily come out across some boggy meadow thickly studded with the sky-blue blossoms of the fringed gentian. Whatever time in the flowering season it may be that our bog walker goes in to explore he is sure to find something worth the search.

Framing the continent, on both east and west, are the long shorelines of the oceans, the Atlantic and the Pacific, and along these shores grow plants as special as any in the land. These are salt-loving or salt-tolerant plants that can live right in the salt water or within range of the ocean spray. Such are the vigorous cord grasses that wave above high tide on the miles and miles of salt marshes or the sea lavender which in the east graces the same marshes with its dainty purple blooms. There are sea asters and sea goldenrod that bloom on the marshes at the very edge of the high tide line and there is the samphire which, though obscurely green in the green marsh during the summer, sets acres afire with its red exuberance in the fall. The seashore lungwort spreads out its fleshy leaves and flaunts its blue flowers along rocks so close to the tumbling waves that you wonder how it can possibly escape destruction. And only slightly less exposed on the sea cliffs above are the thick leaves and yellow, orange and purple-tinted flowers of the roseroot sedum. In the early spring those who dwell upon the coast of British Columbia revel in the pink warmth that the sea blush spreads upon seaside ledges and bluffs and in the sky-blue pattern that blue-eyed Mary lays beside it. So, the seashores, like all the other wet places, have a peculiar floral beauty all their own that no one interested in flowers will fail to investigate.

Buttonbush
Cephalanthus occidentalis
RUBIACEAE

On the edge of a shady swamp in summer you may come upon bushes that seem to be festooned with white spiked balls. These are the 'buttons' of the buttonbush, an elegant decoration of our wetlands. The spikes arise from tiny, fragrant flowers that are crowded on the ball or button. The leaves, either paired and opposite, or in whorls of three or four on the stems, give a lush green setting to the showy buttons. Commonly three to ten feet in height, these sturdy bushes may reach as high as twenty feet in southern swamps.

Curiously, they are robust relatives of fragile bluets and the creeping partridge berry. Its name, *Cephalanthus*, means flowering head.

The buttonbush is occasionally planted as an ornamental shrub, a recognition of its attractive foliage and flowers. It is also browsed by white-tailed deer, antelope and beaver, while its seeds provide food for waterfowl.

Blooms June to August (all year in the far south) in wooded swamps, often in water, and damp swales, occasionally in dry barrens from New Brunswick, Quebec and Ontario south to Florida, Texas, Arizona and California.

Western Skunk Cabbage, Swamp Lantern
Lysichitum americanum

ARACEAE

Very early in the year the golden spathes of this large flower may be seen in the swamps. As the spathes begin to fade the oval leaves develop and become very large. They have been measured fifty-five inches long and thirty inches wide. The flowers are small and green, clustered around a club-like spadix within the golden spathe. The two- to three-foot long flower stalk and leaves grow from a large fleshy root. When crushed, all parts of the plant produce a skunk-like odour.

This is regarded as an edible plant in spite of its odour. The young leaves can be used as a vegetable, if the water in which they are cooked is changed several times. The root was roasted in pits by the Indians who are said to have found it very good. When roasted it could be dried and ground into a flour. Its slightly bitter acrid taste disappeared, if the flour was kept for several weeks before being used. Bears may eat the whole plant, and deer nibble the leaves. The name of the genus is from the Greek meaning a loose cloak, perhaps referring to the large open spathe.

Blooms from February to June in swampy ground along the Pacific coast from Alaska south through British Columbia to northern California, east to Montana.

Canadian Primrose
Primula mistassinica

PRIMULACEAE

The conspicuous yellow eye in the centre of
this flower has earned it another name,
bird's-eye primrose, which is also the name of
the European *P. farinosa*. Calcareous rocks
and clayey soils on wet shores are its preferred habitat.

Primula means first — supposedly the first
to bloom. Mistassinica is the name of a lake
in northern Quebec where it was discovered
by André Michaux, a French botanist.
Michaux was sent to North America by King
Louis XVI of France in 1785 to find suitable
plants for the gardens at Versailles. He called
our species the fairy primrose, because it was
small in size and grew only four to ten inches
tall.

Blooms from May to August along damp
shores from Labrador to Alaska and south to
British Columbia and the northeastern states
of the United States.

Michigan Lily
Lilium michiganense

LILIACEAE

Closely related to the Canada lily and the
Turk's cap lily, it is sometimes mistaken for
either one. It resembles the Turk's cap more
closely, both having well-reflexed petals with
brown spots. In rich wet soil, such as bogs,
wet meadows and woods, it grows to a
height of six feet.

The Turk's cap lily bulbs were reported by
Thoreau to be used to thicken soups. There
are too few of any of these lilies now to use
them in that way, for they are becoming
increasingly rare. These are endangered
species of wildflowers, and we must protect
them.

Blooms from June to August in Ontario
and Manitoba, and south to Tennessee.

Lance-leaved White Violet
Viola lanceolata

VIOLACEAE

Of the many species of white violets in eastern North America, this is probably one of the easiest to identify because of its long, narrow, lance-shaped leaves (*lanceolata*). The flowers bloom on stems two to six inches tall. The three lower petals are purple-veined, the two lateral ones being usually beardless. It produces many seeds like most violets.

This is a stemless violet. Other common white violets are, *V. canadensis*, *V. blanda* and *V. pallens*.

Blooms from March to early July along streams, in wet meadows and bogs, from Nova Scotia to British Columbia and south to California in the west and Florida in the east.

Leatherleaf
Chamaedaphne calyculata

ERICACEAE

Venturing into an open sphagnous bog in spring, the walker may find himself wading through breast-high tangles of graceful dark-leaved branches, each bedecked on its underside with a long line of little white bells. This is the leatherleaf, a bog-loving member of the heath family, whose flowers show its relationship to the better-known blueberry and to the bog rosemary. Ecologically it belongs to a group of shrubs that invade and often overrun sphagnous bogs, ultimately having to give way themselves when still taller shrubs and trees come in and cut down the amount of light available.

The generic name, *Chamaedaphne*, means laurel on the ground. It is misleading as, strictly speaking, it is not a laurel though it is a relative, and some laurels are more low-growing than this plant.

Blooms March to July in peaty bogs and swales from Newfoundland to Alaska, south to New Jersey, to Georgia in the mountains, Ohio, Iowa, Alberta and British Columbia; Eurasia, circumpolar.

Chocolate Lily,
Checker Lily, Riceroot
Fritillaria lanceolata

LILIACEAE

Though its brown mottled colour is not striking, it does attract attention because it is
unusual. This lily is frequently found in open
woods and wet meadows in the west. It was
first discovered by David Douglas in California about 1825. The flower stem reaches a
height of two and a half feet, growing from a
bulbous root which resembles rice grains
stuck together — hence one of its common
names.

Fritillaria is from the Latin *fritillus*, meaning a dice-box, and referring to the dot markings on the flowers. *Lanceolata* means spear-
shaped, which describes the leaves. Western
North America has a large number of wild
fritillarias, of which the most common are *F.
pudica*, *F. atropurpurea*, and *F. camchatcen-
sis*. The Persian fritillary, *F. imperialis*, is a
well-known garden flower.

Blooms from March to June from California to British Columbia.

Canada Holly, Winterberry
Ilex verticillata

AQUIFOLIACEAE

Gleaming scarlet against a blue October sky, lighting up a dark woodland glade, reflected in the dark water lapping the shore of some northern lake—however they are seen, the brilliant red berries of the Canada holly are among the brightest jewels of nature's autumnal crown. The tiny green-white blooms of springtime, concealed in a profusion of leaves, may well be overlooked; but the scarlet berries of the fall leap to the eye, and are a constant source of delight. The ancient Latin name of *Ilex* was once used for the holly oak but is now reserved for the holly genus. The name, *verticillata*, refers to the whorled arrangement of the flowers.

They are equally the joy of many birds: thrushes, robins, bluebirds, catbirds, thrashers and many others feed on them so eagerly that the berries rarely persist long into the winter, despite the common name of winterberry. This shrub, which grows from three to twelve feet high, has been used as an ornamental tree, and as a means of attracting birds in suitably wet gardens.

Blooms June to August in swamps, damp thickets and lake margins (the fruit is most prominent after the leaves fall), from Newfoundland, Ontario and Minnesota south to Georgia, Tennessee and Missouri.

Arrowhead
Sagittaria latifolia
ALISMATACEAE

Rising in groups of three amidst bright green, arrow-shaped leaves, the white flowers of the arrowhead, whether a few inches or two or three feet above water or mud, are always conspicuous. The leaves vary from broad to very narrow but always retain the arrow shape that gives the plant its name of *Sagittaria* or arrowhead. Several closely related species occur.

The arrowheads have long been highly prized by the Indians who collect their tubers either by loosening them with sticks or by treading them out under water with their toes until they float to the top and can be retrieved. Lewis and Clark, in their journey through the Rockies to the Pacific in 1805–6, found these tubers to be the chief vegetable food of the Indians on the Lower Columbia and they themselves lived largely on them during one winter. Among animals both the beaver and the muskrat are very fond of these 'duck potatoes.'

Blooms from July to September in water and wet places from New Brunswick to southern British Columbia, south to South Carolina, Louisiana and California. The similar *S. cuneata* has a more northerly distribution from Quebec to the Mackenzie River and British Columbia, east to Nova Scotia, and south to New England, Indiana and California.

Large Blue Flag, Wild Iris
Iris versicolor

IRIDACEAE

This common wild iris has showy flowers that bloom on stems two to three feet tall. The three sepals are larger than the three erect petals, and are strikingly veined with deep purple on yellow near the centre. The large blue flag can only be pollinated by insects because of the position of the stamens whose pollen cannot reach the pistil without insect help. Bees are said to be fond of blue flowers and wherever there is a group of blue iris, bees can be seen pushing their way beneath the petal-like standard, following the guidelines of the sepals to reach the nectar.

Iris is the name of the Greek goddess of the rainbow. One of the related wild iris of France was chosen by Louis VII as his emblem and became known as the fleur-de-lis (flower of Louis). Later it became the 'Lily of France' and France's emblem.

There are several species of blue iris in North America. *Iris versicolor* is northern in distribution; *I. virginica* is more southern but hybridizes with its northern cousin wherever they meet. The yellow iris, *I. pseudacorus*, has been imported from Europe and become wild in a few locations.

Blooms from May to August in wet meadows and by the shores of lakes and rivers from Labrador to Ontario and Manitoba and south to Virginia.

Grass Pink, Calopogon
Calopogon pulchellus
ORCHIDACEAE

Hidden beneath larch and swamp-loving shrubs such as the leatherleaf, insects must be attracted to this orchid by its vivid colour, for it has no scent. Its lip is at the top, not, as in most orchids, at the bottom. Flying in, the bee lands on the bearded underside and its weight activates the hinge at the base of the lip, allowing it to drop down, so that the bee's back falls on top of the column. The insect's struggles to turn over cause the pollen sacs to break and the pollen grains to adhere to the insect, ready for the next flower.

Calopogon is from the Greek, meaning beautiful beard, and *pulchellus* means pretty. The single grasslike leaf and the flower stalk grow from a tuber which is usually embedded in sphagnum or peat. Offsets from the tuber as well as seeds allow this plant to reproduce and sometimes to increase in numbers, as long as its habitat remains undisturbed. Like many orchids, it requires cool acid bog conditions and can be destroyed by picking. For those who have seen this lovely flower in its natural home, the memory of its beauty is worth more than a dead flower in the hand.

Blooms from May to July from Newfoundland to Minnesota, and south to Florida and Texas.

Swamp Candles,
Yellow Loosestrife
Lysimachia terrestris

PRIMULACEAE

The origin of the generic name is said to be a legend about King Lysimachus of Thrace, who, when chased by a maddened bull, seized a plant of loosestrife and in desperation waved it in front of the animal, thus pacifying him. Another legend tells that oxen were made gentle and submissive if loosestrife was fastened to the tongue of the cart. Both are interesting reasons for the unusual name.

Swamp candles thrive in wet ground. The bright flowers grow as high as three feet.

Blooms from July to September in southeastern Canada and the eastern United States.

Fragrant White Water Lily
Nymphaea odorata

NYMPHAEACEAE

Floating serenely upon polished, quiet water, the many-petalled bowls of the water lily are among the most elegant ornaments of the flower world. The white flowers, one to four inches across, ride among the lily pads, which in this species are green on top and purple underneath. Summer morning air (for these are morning flowers) is often redolent with their perfume. Frogs, small birds, dragonflies and other creatures use the lily pads as convenient resting places and lookout points, so making the lilies a centre for the rich and varied life of a pond or marsh. Though the commoner species is strongly fragrant there is another species, *N. tuberosa*, that is almost or wholly odourless; it grows over a large part of the same range, has wider and more rounded petals and leaves that are usually green underneath.

To this same genus belongs the famous lotus of ancient Egyptian and Greek mythology — symbol of dreamy contentment, a mood that could well describe the feeling of many a summer watcher by a lily-clad pool.

Blooms from June to September in quiet waters from Newfoundland to Manitoba and south to the Gulf of Mexico.

Yellow Pond Lily
Nuphar polysepalum

NYMPHAEACEAE

Like golden balls, the yellow pond lilies rise above the dark waters of bogland pools or quiet streams, set in the midst of mats of broad, heart-shaped lily pads. The three- to five-inch flowers, with their intriguing, umbrella-like stigmas, are unmistakable. This is a western species, having more of the coloured sepals than its kin; but there are several other species, all very much alike, distributed across the continent.

The large, thick rhizomes or underground stems, which may be as much as four or five inches thick and ten feet long, are prized food for the black bear, beaver and moose. They have served as famine fare for the Indians who also collect and roast the large seeds or grind them into meal for bread. The large floating leaves provide platforms for green frogs, dragonflies, ducklings and other denizens of the wild.

Blooms May to August in fairly deep water, always still and quiet, from Alaska south to California, east to Colorado and South Dakota.

Sheep Laurel
Kalmia angustifolia

ERICACEAE

Clusters of cupped, rose-pink blooms, always topped by jaunty shoots of shiny green leaves, distinguish this two- to five-foot shrub from its near relatives among the laurels, the mountain laurel and the bog laurel. In its proper habitats it is often so common as to turn an otherwise bleak landscape into a natural garden. Yet it is feared by farmers since it is poisonous to livestock and sheep, hence its common names of sheep laurel and lambkill. In northern Quebec the plant is so widespread that it can become a major obstacle to the clearing of the land, the tangled roots of the laurel interfering seriously with the passage of the plough.

The generic name, *Kalmia*, commemorates Peter Kalm, a student of the famous Swedish botanist, Linnaeus, who travelled widely in the English American colonies and in New France during the eighteenth century in search of new wild flowers, many of which he sent back to Europe.

Blooms from late May to August in a variety of situations, both wet and dry but preferably acid soils, often in old pastures, sandy barrens and bogs, from Newfoundland and Labrador to Manitoba (Hudson Bay) south to Virginia, Georgia and Michigan.

Broad-leaved Stonecrop
Sedum spathulifolium

CRASSULACEAE

The spray of the Pacific Ocean often wets the rocks where the stonecrop grows. It brightens the shore with its yellow flowers and the reddish stems which support them. *Sedum* is from the Latin verb, to sit, referring to the way in which these succulent plants squat on the rocks of their preferred habitat. The thumb-shaped (*spathulifolium*) thick leaves which form small rosettes at the base are varied in colour, sometimes green, rose, or even lavender. Very young leaves are edible raw or cooked, and have been used in the treatment of wounds. When mature they are bitter-tasting. The flower stalk rises three to twelve inches above the leaves.

Blooms from May to August from British Columbia to California.

Pickerel Weed
Pontederia cordata

PONTEDERIACEAE

Like blue stars on luxuriant green spikes, the blossoms of the pickerel weed embellish stream edges and ponds in late summer. The six-parted flowers, an inch or so across, rest upon dense spikes about five inches long. The whole plant rises from twelve to eighteen inches above the water and is usually accompanied by a single, broad, heart-shaped leaf. As it often appears in great colonies, pickerel weed may fill a whole cove or edge a lake for a long distance.

The name *Pontederia* was given to honour a Professor Giulio Pontedera at the University of Padua in the eighteenth century.

Pickerel use such beds as hiding places and are said to lay their eggs on the underwater parts of these plants by preference. It has been frequently used as a water garden ornamental plant and is a close relative of the well-known water hyacinth of the southern states. Polluted water has caused its decline in some areas.

Blooms June to November in quiet, shallow water or in mud from Nova Scotia to Minnesota, south to Florida and Texas.

Cardinal Flower
Lobelia Cardinalis

CAMPANULACEAE

No flower growing in the wet places is more striking to the eye than the unmistakable scarlet cardinal flower, one of the glories of late summer. Growing as high as five or six feet in favourable situations, it is conspicuous in dark swamps and on the verges of ponds and streams. Early explorers and settlers from Europe were quick to appreciate its beauty, for it was one of the first North American flowers to be taken back to England for use in gardens, being known there in Queen Elizabeth I's time. Its bright red blooms are favourites with nectar-seeking hummingbirds and the larger butterflies. The plant got its specific name from the resemblance of the corolla to a bishop's mitre and of the red of the flower to a cardinal's robe. We are told that the Indians made both a cough medicine and a love potion from this plant. The generic name, *Lobelia*, commemorates Matthias de l'Obel, a Flemish herbalist of the sixteenth century.

Blooms from late July through September in swampy woods, along damp shores and sluggish streams and in wet meadows from New Brunswick to southern Ontario and Michigan and south to the Gulf of Mexico.

Water Arum, Wild Calla
Calla palustris

ARACEAE

Sometimes, the eye-catching white spathes of the water arum may cover an open boggy pool; at other times, it will be found blooming in solitary splendour in some sunlit swampy corner. The specific name refers to its marshy habitat. Inside its greeny-white spathe, one to three inches in size, nestles a flower-studded spadix, while above and behind rise broad, heart-shaped leaves. The fruit is a cluster of red berries.

The wild calla, though smaller, resembles the florist's calla, a plant which belongs to the same family but which comes from a quite different genus. Both berries and underground parts of this plant have been used by Indians as food in spite of the fiery-hot chemicals it contains. In northern Europe the rhizomes (underground stems) have been ground into flour to make bread.

Blooms from April to August in bogs, swamps and shallow water from Newfoundland across Canada to British Columbia and Alaska, south to New Jersey, Pennsylvania, Indiana and Minnesota. Also in Eurasia as this is a circumpolar species.

Rhodora
Rhododendron canadense

ERICACEAE

Introduction to rhodora could well come as one is driving along a springtime road in the Maritimes or Maine and suddenly sees half a landscape suffused in mauve or rose-purple. The massed blooms seem unbelievable until one wanders among the flower-laden shrubs that are one to three feet high and finds himself quite surrounded. The bushes may also grow singly but, single or massed, rhodora offers one of the greatest floral shows of northeastern North America. The dark, shiny green or grey-green foliage comes chiefly after the blooms. The flowers of this rhododendron resemble those of the azalea members of this genus. In their early blooming they are the haunt of bumblebees.

Ralph Waldo Emerson was so impressed with the rhodora that he referred to it frequently in his poetry. The plant has also given its name as title to a well-known botanical journal.

Blooms from March to July, sometimes September, in bogs, wet woods, damp thicket-strewn meadows and acid barrens from Newfoundland, southern Quebec and northern New York south to New Jersey and eastern Pennsylvania.

Water Smartweed
Polygonum coccineum

POLYGONACEAE

The bright pink spikes of water smartweed reflected in the dark water make it one of the most distinctive of aquatic plants. A very variable species, it grows sometimes half-submerged with floating leaves; yet it is often found in shore mud or on a half-dried marsh. Its leaves and flower heads vary in shape and size according to its habitat; the plant that spreads low when resting upon the water, for instance, becomes quite erect when growing in exposed mud. A similar species (*P. amphibium*) has similar habits, but usually has flower heads that are thick and stubby, an inch or less in length as compared to the longer and slenderer ones of this species.

The generic name, *Polygonum*, means many knees or joints, describing the swollen joints common to the genus. The specific name, *coccineum*, refers to this species' red colour. The seeds of the water smartweeds are an important source of food for wild ducks.

Blooms from June to September in shallow water, muddy shores, marshes, swamps and meadows from Nova Scotia and Quebec to British Columbia, south to North Carolina, Arkansas, Texas and California.

Touch-me-not, Jewelweed
Impatiens capensis

BALSAMINACEAE

Glowing against a background of dark, damp thickets or overhanging water, the touch-me-not, with its red-spotted orange flowers, is always conspicuous. Two to five feet tall and often heavily massed as well as profuse in bloom, it is a striking plant. The flowers develop into enticing green capsules that explode at a touch when ripe, projecting their seeds all around. It is these pods that earn for the plant its common name of touch-me-not as well as its Latin name, *Impatiens*.

The juice of the plant is widely used in folk medicine as a protection against and a relief for poison ivy rash. The flowers attract hummingbirds, bumblebees and honeybees in their search for nectar. Taken to England as a garden plant, it has become naturalized there under the name American jewelweed.

Blooms from June to September in low, wet and springy places from Newfoundland and Quebec to Saskatchewan and south to South Carolina, Alabama and Oklahoma. It may be found in various colour forms.

American Speedwell,
American Brooklime, Veronica
Veronica americana

SCROPHULARIACEAE

This charming blue flower bears the name of St. Veronica. An early Christian legend relates that St. Veronica wiped the face of Jesus on the way to Calvary with her handkerchief which, thereafter, retained a *vera iconica*, a true image of his features.

A common genus of the northern hemishere, there are many species in North America. The most widespread are the American speedwell, *Veronica americana*, *V. scutellata* and *V. persica*. The stem may reach a height of three feet, but is usually only six to twelve inches high.

The common name, speedwell, was an old English term used in the same way as 'God be with you.' To present a departing guest with a sprig of speedwell was to wish him a safe journey.

Blooms from June to August in wet places and swamps, from Newfoundland to Alaska, and south to California.

Blueberry
Vaccinium angustifolium

ERICACEAE

In summer, the clusters of luscious blue berries on this plant are familiar enough; less well known are the little bell-like pink or white flowers which come in spring. This is the low sweet blueberry, a freely branching shrub that grows from two inches to a foot or so high, with lance-shaped green leaves. It may spread over wide areas of dry or rocky soil and in peat bogs, known as blueberry barrens, where in fall its foliage makes a brilliant show of red. There are many other kinds of blueberries, ranging across the continent, from ground-hugging types in the Arctic to high bush species that may become small trees in the south. The generic name, *Vaccinium*, apparently refers to cows and to their being pastured in areas where such berries were common.

The berries are a favourite food of many animals, especially bears, and birds. They are used both fresh and dried by the Indians and as a favourite pie filling throughout North America.

Blooms May to July on dry, rocky or sandy barrens and peat bogs (fruit: June to August) from Labrador and Newfoundland to Saskatchewan, south to Virginia, Ohio and Iowa.

Rose Pogonia
Pogonia ophioglossoides

ORCHIDACEAE

The delicately perfumed, nodding pink head of the rose pogonia with its fringed and bearded lip is one of the joys of the sphagnum bog. It often grows together with other orchids like calopogon and arethusa. It may be distinguished from the latter, which it somewhat resembles, by its broad, sheathing leaf placed well up the stem. It is frequently found in good-sized colonies as a result of its habit of vigorous underground growth through spreading rhizomes (underground stems). Occasional white-flowered forms occur.

The generic name, *Pogonia*, means bearded. The specific name, *ophioglossoides*, means 'like a serpent's tongue,' hence another common name, snakemouth. Although taken from North America and introduced into English gardens about 1815, it has proved to be difficult to grow in cultivation. Hence, its fragile beauty is best left to its wild haunts.

Blooms May to August in bogs, wet meadows and shores from Newfoundland to Ontario and Minnesota, south to Pennsylvania, Tennessee and Missouri, on the coastal plain to Florida and Texas.

Showy or
Queen Lady's Slipper
Cypripedium reginae

ORCHIDACEAE

Whether gracing the sun-dappled shadows of some tangled bog or cascading in massive bloom in an open swamp, this noblest of northern orchids is highly prized wherever it grows. The prominent rose and white slippers, up to an inch and a half long, ride upon plants that may be as much as three feet or more tall.

The generic name, *Cypripedium*, means Aphrodite's slipper, the goddess who was said to have been born on the island of Cyprus.

So attractive is this plant that it has suffered badly from overpicking and attempted transplanting. It does not do well in gardens as a rule and should be left in its natural surroundings unmolested. In many places it is a protected plant and protection should be extended further as it is severely threatened. For some people handling this plant produces a rash similar to that from poison ivy. This is the provincial flower of Prince Edward Island and the state flower of Minnesota.

Blooms from May to August in swamps, mossy bogs, damp woods and shores from Newfoundland to Manitoba, south to New Jersey, the mountains of Georgia and Tennessee, and Missouri.

Marsh Marigold, King-cup, Cowslip
Caltha palustris

RANUNCULACEAE

> And winking Mary-buds begin
> To ope their golden eyes
> > Shakespeare: 'Hark, hark, the lark'

This favourite flower has so many common names that it is impossible to list them all. How gaily it brightens our marshes and borders our small streams in springtime! As its species name implies, it lives only in wet places, growing to over two feet after flowering. *Palustris* means marsh-loving. *Caltha* is the Latin name for the true marigold (from *calathos*, a cup), and was transferred to the unrelated marsh marigold. The petals of these flowers produce a yellow dye.

Though the plant is highly poisonous when raw, it is safe to use when boiled. The flower buds and the leaves are the parts used, and are reported to taste better than spinach.

Blooms through April to June from Labrador to Alaska and south throughout most of the United States. Also in England and Europe, as well as Asia.

Broad-leaved Cattail
Typha latifolia

TYPHACEAE

The familiar tall brown cattails that stand in clumps among their sword-like leaves in our marshes are in reality the fruiting masses of myriads of tiny flowers. Light-coloured spikes of the male or staminate flowers occur above the larger cattails in the spring but are seldom noticed; they fall off as soon as they drop their pollen, leaving only the bare spike. Eventually the cattail becomes a mass of fluff-cloaked nutlets that fly about the countryside, settling where they can. A similar but narrow-leaved species (*T. angustifolia*) may also be found. The generic name, *Typha*, is the ancient Greek name for the same plant. *Latifolia*, the specific name, means broad-leaved.

The cattail has been widely used for many purposes: its roots for flour, its young shoots and flower heads as vegetables, its leaves for basketry, matting and chair-making, and its down as wound-dressing and packing. The roots are highly prized as food by muskrats and geese, and many birds and animals use the cattail marshes for nesting and shelter.

Blooms May to July in marshes throughout North America. Also in Europe and Asia.

Arethusa
Arethusa bulbosa

ORCHIDACEAE

This rare and beautiful orchid is a true bog plant. Named arethusa in honour of an ancient Greek wood-nymph, it occurs typically in deep sphagnum moss amidst heathy shrubs. Rising from a few inches to a foot or more above its base, the stalk bears a single large bloom, rarely two, of arching magenta petals and sepals, with a pendant lip bearing three yellow or white hairy ridges. This latter is so like an animal's lolling tongue that this orchid is often mistaken for its relative, the snakemouth or rose pogonia. The pogonia is distinguishable from the arethusa by its ovate or elliptic leaf midway up the stem.

Arethusa is said to have been used in the past as a remedy for toothache. Unfortunately this lovely flower is now approaching extinction in more populated areas. It should never be picked or removed.

Blooms from May to August in sphagnous bogs and peaty meadows from Newfoundland to Ontario and Manitoba, south to Maryland, the mountains of South Carolina, and in Ohio, Indiana and Wisconsin.

Purple Loosestrife
Lythrum salicaria

LYTHRACEAE

A marsh converted to a purple pond, a fountain of purple upon a riverbank, or a column of purple in the swamp, all indicate the presence of that world traveller, the purple loosestrife. Brought to North America from Europe, it has become aggressively at home and now flourishes in wet places throughout the eastern part of the continent. The tall, handsome plants may grow up to six feet and have flowering heads a foot or more in length.

The generic name, *Lythrum*, goes back to the classical Greek, and refers to this same plant. The specific name, *salicaria*, means like a willow and applies to the leaves.

Purple loosestrife is greatly prized as a garden plant. It was also made the subject of intensive study in the last century by Charles Darwin, who was interested in its ingenious method of cross-fertilization. This plant is favoured by all manner of insects, bumblebees, bees, flies and butterflies.

Blooms from June to September in marshes, swamps and wet meadows from Newfoundland and Quebec to Minnesota, south to Virginia, Ohio and Missouri. Also in Europe, Asia, North Africa and Australia.

Canada Anemone
Anemone canadensis

RANUNCULACEAE

The sight of the snowy banks of this gregarious anemone is a sure sign that spring is well launched. Common and striking, it can hardly be missed on damp slopes and in wet hollows. Its white flowers, an inch or more across, topping stalks that rise out of a circle of stemless leaves at the middle of the plant, may be a few inches or two feet above the ground. The leaves are deeply cut, being five- to seven-parted, and are sharply toothed. Those at the base have long petioles or 'stems.' It is one of our tallest anemones.

The ancient name, *Anemone*, is a corruption of the semitic *Na'man*, meaning Adonis, from whose blood the brilliant red anemone of the Middle East was said to have arisen.

This native plant, now widely used as a garden plant, has escaped into areas not previously occupied by it. The Indians had various ways of using it in their folk medicine.

Blooms May to July in moist meadows, on damp slopes and along streambanks from Labrador to Alberta, south to Maryland, West Virginia, Indiana, Kansas and New Mexico.

Blue Camas, Common Camas
Camassia quamash

LILIACEAE

At one time, in early summer the high wet meadows of the west used to be blue with this flower. It was described by Lewis and Clark in the journal of their expedition of 1805. The bulbs grew in such quantities that they formed an important part of the diet of the West Coast Indians before the white population covered this region. Now they can only be seen in such numbers in national parks and other sanctuaries. There is a Camas Valley in Oregon, and the old Indian name for Fort Victoria (now Victoria), on Vancouver Island, was Camosun or 'the place for gathering camas.' The name is said to be a corruption of an Indian word *chamas*, meaning sweet. Sometimes a kind of molasses was made from boiling the bulbs, which were gathered after the flowers had fallen. Occasionally a similar bulb, common in the same places, was gathered by mistake. This bulb, belonging to the death camas, *Zygadenus gramineus*, is highly poisonous to both humans and cattle.

A closely related species, *C. leichtlinii*, may be found over much the same range in the west, growing to a similar height of about three feet. In the southeastern United States, *C. hyacinthina* has a pale blue flower and is similar in habitat and appearance, though smaller.

Blooms from April to July in high wet areas from British Columbia to California and east to Montana, Wyoming and Utah.

47

Elephant's Head
Pedicularis groenlandica

SCROPHULARIACEAE

The writer of an old herbal, John Gerard, states that the louseworts were plants which 'fill sheep and other cattle that feed in the meadows where it groweth full of lice'! This is one of the louseworts of which there are many around the world. Hence comes the generic name from the Latin *pediculus*, meaning louse. *Groenlandica* means from Greenland. Our species, though a member of this genus, is not commonly called lousewort, but elephant's head, due to the shape of the small flowers, easily seen in this picture. These are the only real pink elephants! When in need of food northern people used the leaves for tea and the boiled roots for a vegetable.

Usually found in wet meadows and on the shores of mountain lakes and streams, it grows to a height of two feet with fernlike leaves.

Blooms from June to August from Labrador to Alaska, in the mountains of British Columbia and Alberta and south to California and Colorado.

Salmonberry
Rubus spectabilis
ROSACEAE

A showy shrub, both in flower and in fruit, it is aptly named *spectabilis*. The generic name *rubus* means red and describes the fruit of many of the species. The flower blooms very early at sea level, and may still be found in bloom at high altitudes into August. The berries may ripen early, look like large raspberries in shape, and are sweet and juicy to eat. The shrub grows in damp woods, swamps, and along banks of streams, to a height of twelve feet. The canes or branches have many short prickles.

Young shoots of this plant are edible, and the fruit is a rich source of Vitamin C. Both shoots and fruit were eaten by the West Coast Indians, as reported by David Douglas in his diary of his trip on the Columbia River in 1825.

Blooms from February to August from Alaska to California, on the west side of the coastal mountains.

Great Blue Lobelia
Lobelia siphilitica

CAMPANULACEAE

The great blue lobelia may be found in two different forms: as a tall stand of brilliant blooms at the edge of a wooded swamp, or as mounds of blue close to the ground in some open, spongy bog. Wherever seen or whatever the size, it is the blue counterpart of its close relative, the red cardinal flower. It is easy to see why many successful attempts have been made to grow this conspicuous plant in wet-soil gardens.

Its Latin name indicates that it was once used as a cure for syphilis. Some of the afflicted are said to have bought this 'secret remedy' from the Indians in the eighteenth century though, like so many other elements of medical folklore, it has been long forgotten and has no support in modern medicine.

Blooms from August to October in rich, low woods, swamps, other wet lands and roadside ditches from Maine to southern Ontario and Manitoba south to North Carolina, Alabama and Texas.

Bottle Gentian, Closed Gentian
Gentiana andrewsii

GENTIANACEAE

Looking for all the world like a cluster of dark purple-blue Christmas tree lights, the inch-long blooms of the bottle gentian sit on their underpinning of leafy green, a foot or two above meadow or bog. With their closed appearance, it is a puzzle how these flowers can be fertilized. In full sunlight, however, this flower does open sufficiently for a short time to allow bumblebees to enter, if with difficulty, and perform the necessary fertilization. Occasionally the flowers occur in pink or pure white.

This is one of the unmistakable beauties of the late summer scene. Despite the production of a large amount of seed it is rarely abundant in any one place. The name *Gentiana* refers to Gentius, King of Illyria, who discovered the medicinal value of the gentians according to the Roman writer Pliny. This species is called *andrewsii* after a well-known English botanical artist of the early nineteenth century.

Blooms in meadows, bogs, damp prairies, edges of wet woods from Quebec to Saskatchewan, south to Georgia, Arkansas and Nebraska.

Pitcher Plant
Sarracenia purpurea

SARRACENIACEAE

The pitcher plant, with its umbrella-like flowers, of purple, wine-red or yellow-green, grows on stems twelve to twenty inches high. Nodding above circles of pitcher-shaped, hollow leaves, all veined in red, green and purple, it is one of the best-known sights in Canadian bogs. These hollow leaves are lined with down-pointing bristles, facilitating the downward passage of insects that alight on them and making their upward return difficult or impossible so that the insects drown and are digested in the watery liquid that is usually present at the bottom of the leaves. Thus we have here a characteristic example of a carnivorous plant.

Discovered in Canada in the seventeenth century by Dr. Michel Sarrasin of Quebec, the plant's Latin name was given to honour its discoverer. Today the pitcher plant is the provincial floral emblem of Newfoundland. The Indians commonly considered it a good remedy for smallpox, though there is no scientific proof of this.

Blooms from late May to August in sphagnum bogs and peat barrens from Newfoundland and Labrador across northern Canada to the Mackenzie River region and south to Maryland, Ohio and Minnesota.

Red or Pink Monkey Flower
Mimulus lewisii

SCROPHULARIACEAE

The lovely colour of the flower of this perennial attracts attention along the high mountain streams, on wet rocky slopes and in ditches, throughout western North America. It often grows in large clumps, up to two and a half feet high.

The Latin for mimic was used to create the generic name, because the corolla, in some species, looks like the face of a monkey. The specific name honours Captain Meriwether Lewis, secretary to President Thomas Jefferson, and leader with William Clark of the famous expedition sent out to explore the far west of America. Lewis is reported to have found the plant near the present site of Glacier National Park in 1805.

There are many species of *Mimulus* in North America, mostly in the west. Two common ones, *M. moschatus* and *M. guttatus* have bright yellow flowers. The eastern monkey flower, *M. ringens*, is a violet blue and grows along the shores of lakes and rivers.

Blooms in July and August, throughout western North America.

Fringed Gentian
Gentiana crinita

GENTIANACEAE

Scattered through the meadows in autumn are the misty blue blossoms of the fringed gentian. Sometimes they hug the ground; sometimes they raise their urn-shaped blooms along spreading branches as much as three feet high, forming a delicate candelabra. Lovers of sunshine, they open widely only on sunny days, remaining tightly closed on dull, dark days as if in protest against the gloom. They vary greatly in the tone of blue they present, from very light to dark and purplish, the lighter being commoner.

The gentian family is named after King Gentius of Illyria, who discovered that certain gentians had medicinal value.

Blooms from late August to November in meadows, damp woods and bogs from Maine to Ontario and Manitoba and south to Georgia, Ohio, Indiana and Iowa. Similar to the narrow-leaved fringed gentian (*Gentiana procera*) which extends from New York, the midwest and southern Ontario to Alaska.

Jack-in-the-Pulpit
Arisaema triphyllum

ARACEAE

Standing erect beneath a colourful over-arching back a foot or two above the ground, Jack does indeed appear to be preaching to a Lilliputian congregation from an old-fashioned pulpit. The Jack is the flowering spadix and the arching back the spathe of this plant. The latter may be purple, bronze, green or a striped combination of all three colours inside. The large, three-parted leaf is distinctive.

The generic name, *Arisaema*, is derived from the Greek *aris*, another kind of arum, and *haima*, describing the spotted leaves of some species. *Triphyllum* means three-leaved.

As an example of how different peoples see the same object, it is interesting to note that the Iroquois Indians called this plant *Kah-a-hoo-sa*, meaning Indian cradle, apparently because of the resemblance to the carrying rack in which an Iroquois woman carried her baby on her back.

Although intensely burning and poisonous if eaten raw, the corms of the plant are palatable after careful cooking and were widely eaten by the Indians, hence another of the plant's common names, Indian turnip.

Blooms from April to June in moist, rich woods and thickets from New Brunswick and Quebec to Manitoba, south to Florida, Louisiana and Kansas.

The Arctic—Alpine area

There are two ways of reaching Arctic terrain. You may travel many hundreds of miles northward to enter the Arctic zone; or you may climb a few thousand feet up a mountain and emerge upon the arctic-alpine tundra. Granted differences resulting from local conditions, it is roughly true to say that for every forty feet you ascend you will have gone the equivalent of about ten miles north; hence, if you climb 4,000 feet on a mountain you will have proceeded northward a thousand miles. And each 330 feet of altitude brings a drop of one degree in mean temperature, which helps to explain why arctic conditions prevail in the high mountains. In the southern Canadian West, arctic-alpine country begins to appear in the mountains at approximately 5,000 to 7,000 feet, depending upon the local situation, this being affected by wind, snowfall, angle and direction of exposure and other factors. In the western United States to the south it is necessary to climb progressively higher to reach the arctic level, whereas northward it gradually becomes lower until reaches sea level in the Arctic proper.

In eastern North America few mountains reach an altitude that makes an arctic-alpine situation possible. Nonetheless, in the Adirondacks, the Green Mountains and the White Mountains, and on the higher peaks of Maine and the Gaspé Peninsula it does occur. There are, for instance, over 200 species of arctic-alpine plants on the uppermost parts of Mt. Washington, a 6,000-foot peak in New Hampshire. Clearly then, getting up high, holds all sorts of promise to those looking for new and unusual wildflowers.

To the hiker making his way step by step up a twisting mountain trail will come the fullest opportunity to appreciate all the mountain changes. Starting in the woods, he will climb on up, finding surprises at every turn, until he suddenly sees that the trees no longer tower above his head; they have become only as tall as himself. A few more turns and they are only half as tall. They are becoming gnarled, contorted, and almost seem to writhe upon the ground. And as he keeps on up the trail there comes a moment when he sees no evident trees at all; he has come out upon a great meadowland dotted with flowers of yellow and blue, white and red, stretching away to a rim of snowy peaks. Soon he will come to a point where he can look back. Then, as he sees the edge of the stunted woods snaking its way across the landscape below him, mounting up little sheltered valleys, retreating upon open, exposed spurs, he will realize that he has passed the timberline, which he can see is not so much a line as a tattered band.

The timberline is where the arctic-alpine zone begins. It is alpine as well as arctic because studies of this type of country began first in the Alps in Europe and the term 'alpine' came to be applied to similar situations throughout the mountains of the world. Only later did the close relationship between alpine and arctic conditions come to be understood, so the combined name 'arctic-alpine' is now used to describe this type of country.

The magnificent mountain settings of so many arctic-alpine meadows may cause the admiring observer to forget the harsh challenge which this rugged country offers to all life, not least to plant life. In the face of this challenge only the fittest and the best adapted can survive. Above all, plants here must adapt to a short growing season, three months at the most, sometimes as little as eight weeks. They must be able to cope with the bitter cold of a long winter, and they have to withstand the effects of frigid and desiccating winds. Indeed, such winds can be so damaging that open exposure to them can easily be fatal, so that heavy snow cover may be a protective boon for plants even though it may delay their springtime blooming. And seepage from melting snow is always a welcome source of water on these wind-blown heights.

When spring does come to the western mountains, usually towards the end of June, the sight is truly amazing. White and gold avalanche lilies edge the brims of melting snowdrifts, rising up through the snow itself; blue-flushed, cream-coloured western anemones hug the snow in their fuzzy jackets; across the open meadows cascades of almost every shade of colour join with the lilies and the anemones in a flood that reaches away to the horizon. Such sights of alpine meadows are among the great floral experiences of the world and the sudden and nearly simultaneous blooming of all kinds of plants which they represent is one of the crucial adaptations which arctic-alpine plants make to the challenge of their land. Mostly perennials, they are all set to burst into activity at the very first opportunity, even through the snow, to take every advantage of the short growing season.

Another characteristic of arctic-alpine plants is that they are virtually all low-growing or dwarfed. Only in the most sheltered spots are exceptions likely to be found. Moreover, the higher one climbs in the mountains and the more exposed the landscape becomes the more evident is the ground-hugging aspect of the plants. Yet the flowers on these plants are large and richly-coloured beyond all expectation. Nowhere is this more clearly demonstrated than in the lush blooms of the purple saxifrage, the blue alpine forget-me-not and the moss campion.

The campion, with its pink flowers, is also a tempting green cushion, spread across grey rock and anchored in a soil-filled crevice. Beside it may sit what appears to be a green and yellow etching on the grey rock, composed of shining green leaves and yellowish fingers of bloom. It is only a few inches high yet what we are looking at here, far beyond the timberline and despite superficial appearances, is a tree — the arctic willow. If we were to cut through the tiny little 'trunk' and count its rings, we could well find that this dwarf specimen is fifty or a hundred years old. It will never grow any higher but will spread out across the rocky ground. By this low-growing habit arctic-alpine plants can secure protection against the incessant cold winds with their threat of desiccation. To this security, the cushion plants add the capacity to create within their cushions a micro-habitat where the temperature is often several degrees higher than the surrounding air. The disproportionately large flowers offer a special attraction to the none too plentiful insects of this difficult terrain. All these characteristics are ways of meeting the challenge of the environment.

Another answer to this challenge is to be found in the foliage and stems of these plants. Western anemones, bedecked in soft, silky white hairiness, are a perfect example of this. So, too, are the shiny green leaves of the Labrador tea, which are leathery and thick, with rolled-under edges, and are covered underneath with a sort of rusty wool. The mountain heathers, the white, the red and the yellow, which hang their exquisite bells so profusely in the high meadows, also have protective foliage. On the white, the leaves are tiny and scalelike, needle-shaped on the red and gland-covered on the yellow. Hairiness, thickness, leathery surfaces, rolled edges, glandular covering and small-sized leaves are all devices for combatting the cold, for preventing excess evaporation in the desiccating winds and for protection against the intense sunlight of these high parts.

The high meadows of the mountains are in effect southern outposts of that circumpolar world, the Arctic, which caps all the northernmost part of the earth. In the Arctic, with its permafrost, its sodden tundra and its long dark winters, there might appear to be differences of living conditions great enough to make this a wholly different realm. The evidence of the animal population might seem to emphasize the differences, but when one comes to the plants it is to discover that many of the same plants, or very similar species, dwell in both the mountains and the Arctic. The reason for the identity or close similarity among the plants must be that, whatever the differences, the conditions of life are fundamentally the same in both areas. When one thinks of the short growing season, (ameliorated in the Arctic by the long daylight of summer), the cold, the snow and the savage winds, it is possible to see the similarities in habitat. It is therefore not surprising that the same or similar plants, adapting in similar ways, should occupy the Arctic land.

What is more surprising, to those who have never experienced it, is the realization that with the onset of summer the Arctic world bursts into bloom much in the manner of the alpine meadows. Coming then to join the colourful lichens, those most prevalent and most distinctive of Arctic plants, are the yellow drifts of Arctic poppies, the blue splashes of the Arctic lupine and the purple saxifrage. Cotton grass waves in the Arctic winds, while Arctic willows raise roseate spikes into the cool air. Even an azalea, the Alpine azalea, and a rhododendron, the Lapland rosebay, display their pink and rose blossoms upon the Arctic earth. Thus, throughout its few weeks of summer, the Arctic can be a splendidly colourful and flowerful land, full of vigour and life, until the quick autumn in a wave of brilliant red and gold brings summer to a close.

Won against great odds, these wonderful natural gardens, the Arctic and the alpine, are amongst the finest achievements of nature. Fixed in rugged country, successfully meeting the challenges of their environments, they seem sure to be there for our enjoyment forever. Yet, now that our knowledge of them is increasing, we begin to realize how very fragile their situation really is. Man, who brings his animals to graze in the high meadows, who rolls his machinery across the tundra, who builds and camps and tramps, often regardless of the consequences, has manifestly overturned the natural balance in many of these places, and they have begun to die or have gone. It is now evident that unless people are willing to submit to restraints and controls in their use, many of these beautiful Arctic-alpine areas will be doomed to destruction.

Broad Leaved Willow Herb, Mountain Fireweed, River Beauty
Epilobium Latifolium

ONAGRACEAE

Spread as a carpet across open Arctic meadows, or along the gravelly edges of mountain streams, the conspicuous colour of this large flowered relation of the fireweed makes it a breathtaking sight. Its habit of growth is low, usually four to sixteen inches high.

Epilobium is derived from two Greek words meaning upon, and, a pod, referring to the position of the four petals and four sepals above the ovary. *Latifolium* describes the broad lance shaped leaves of this species.

The young shoots and flower buds are edible both raw and cooked. The root has been used, ground up, as a poultice on sores. But as this plant spreads only by seeds, it should be used only in an emergency.

Its range is arctic-alpine and circumpolar. It grows along river bars and on wet gravelly slopes in the mountains, from Greenland across Arctic America and south to Newfoundland, Quebec, Ontario and south in the mountains to Colorado, South Dakota and Oregon. The blooming season extends from June to September.

Tufted Fleabane
Erigeron caespitosus

COMPOSITAE

An attractive plant of the high, dry prairies and the Rocky Mountains, this fleabane grows two to twelve inches high on stems that curve at the bottom, then come erect. The grey-green leaves are broader and more massed near the base, and fewer, narrower and more elongate higher up the stem. The flowering heads may come singly or severally, each one having up to one hundred narrow rays, white, pink or bluish in colour.

The many different kinds of fleabane are closely related to asters and sometimes overlap with them in their characteristics. In general, though, fleabanes bloom earlier, have more numerous and narrower rays and their flower heads are borne on less leafy stems.

The name of fleabane, applied to the entire *Erigeron* group, goes back to the time when fleas were a common human pest and when many plants were used to try to ward them off. The specific name, *caespitosus*, means tufted, hence the common name.

Blooms from June to August in dry, open places from Manitoba to Yukon and Alaska, south to North Dakota, Nebraska, Wyoming and Washington.

Alpine Forget-me-not
Myosotis alpestris
BORAGINACEAE

The deep blue of a northern sky seems caught in the petals of this high mountain flower. It prefers moist meadows and slopes. Never very tall, its height varies from four to twelve inches.

Myosotis means mouse, from the Greek *mus*, and ear from *ous*, referring to the leaf shape in some species. An old legend tells the story of a young man who, while gathering flowers for his sweetheart, slipped and fell into the river. As he was swept away, he tossed the flowers on the bank and cried 'forget-me-not.'

Blooms from June to August in the mountains of Alaska south to British Columbia and Alberta and as far as Oregon and Colorado.

Glacier Lily, Snow Lily
Erythronium grandiflorum

LILIACEAE

Reported by the explorers Lewis and Clark, and introduced into England by David Douglas, the plant hunter, this lovely lily has been known for many years as a close relative of the eastern fawn lily. The flowers are larger and the leaves unspotted. The plant often reaches a height of sixteen inches. It comes up through the snow in the mountains as early as May and can be seen in vast numbers in Glacier National Park, where it was given the common name of glacier lily.

It is said that its bulbs are eaten by bears. The Blackfoot Indians used the root as a treatment for boils and skin sores.

Blooms from May to July in the coastal range from British Columbia to California and east to the Rockies.

Silverberry, Wolf Willow
Elaeagnus commutata

ELEAGNACEAE

The silvery colour of flowers, leaves and fruit of this shrub make it unusual and easily recognized. Its habitat is on dry calcareous slopes along streams and lakesides. The height is from two to twelve feet.

The inconspicuous, pale yellow-lined silver flowers, born in the axils of the leaves, have a strong aromatic fragrance. Thanks to this attraction, insects come quickly to them. It blooms across the prairies when the wild roses are flowering, in early summer. The silver berries are edible though very dry and mealy. They ripen in August. Indian women used to boil off the flesh and reveal the beautiful brown nuts inside. Then a hole was bored through each, and it was strung on to the buckskin fringe of their jackets as decoration and to weight it down. Pioneer women liked to use these nuts for necklaces.

Blooms in June and July from Quebec to Alaska and south to Minnesota and Utah.

Purple Mountain Saxifrage
Saxifraga oppositifolia

SAXIFRAGACEAE

The very tiny flowers, less than a half-inch in diameter, are too vivid in colour to miss when climbing above timberline in the mountains. The flower stems are usually less than one inch long, but may reach a height of two inches in sheltered places. The leaves are very small, too, as one would expect. The whole plant usually forms a mat and clings to the rocks on which it grows, where it is hard to dislodge, in spite of ice, snow and wind. Thus it may survive for years.

Suxifraga is from *saxum*, a stone, and *frangere*, to break. Since this perennial grows in rocky or gravelly places in Alpine areas, it is credited with an ability to 'break rocks,' and its anchoring roots probably assist in this process. It is the only species of this genus which has opposite leaves, hence *oppositifolia*.

Blooms from June to August across the Arctic regions of North America, in the high mountains of Alberta and British Columbia and south to Washington and Wyoming; circumpolar.

Bog Rosemary
Andromeda glaucophylla

ERICACEAE

The shell-pink or white flowers of the bog rosemary usually hide themselves from all save those who penetrate to the wettest open places of sphagnum bogs; yet there are few who do not feel that the sight of such delicate beauty is a satisfying reward for all their effort. Occasionally a highway may pass by or through a suitable bog, as does the Cabot Trail in Cape Breton, Nova Scotia, and then the passerby may see this beauty right beside the road. This small, evergreen shrub, rising a few inches to two and a half feet high, with its narrow, leathery leaves, rolled under and whitened underneath, resembles garden rosemary in general appearance though the flowers are quite different, hence its common name. A close relative, marsh or Arctic bog rosemary, has been used in Europe to make a black dye. This genus is named for the beautiful Greek maiden, Andromeda. The species is named *glaucophylla* for its bluish-green leaves.

Blooms from May to August, sometimes September, from southwestern Greenland and Labrador to Saskatchewan and south to New Jersey, West Virginia, Indiana and Minnesota. Closely similar to Arctic bog rosemary (*A. polifolia*) which is circumpolar in its range across northern Canada, Alaska and Eurasia.

Labrador Tea
Ledum groenlandicum

ERICACEAE

Typical inhabitant of cold, acid bogs, this shrub, up to three or four feet tall, may be known at once by its narrow leaves, with rolled-over edges and under-covering of rusty wool, that are commonly bunched at the ends of twigs. The showy terminal clusters of white, rather open flowers, adorned with protruding stamens, show up against their background of dark, evergreen foliage. The leaves are aromatic when crushed, hence the generic name of *Ledum*. A similar but smaller species (*L. palustre*) occurs in the far north and the two have sometimes been confused.

Learning from the Indians, the *coureurs de bois* and the colonist-settlers used the leaves, crushed and dried, as a substitute for tea, hence the common name.

Blooms May to August in bogs and along wet shores from Greenland and Labrador to Alaska, south to New Jersey, Ohio, Minnesota, Alberta and Washington.

Alp Lily
Lloydia serotina

LILIACEAE

Named after an early Welsh naturalist, Edward Llwyd (1660–1709), this tiny lily lives in Alpine and Arctic areas. The species name *serotina* means late, but this seems incongruous, for the flowers begin to appear in June, which is usual for an Alpine plant. The bulblike roots from which the two- to four-inch flower stem and narrow leaves grow, can be matted together in considerable numbers. It prefers open rocky areas. This is the only species of this genus found in North America.

   Blooms from June to August in Alaska, British Columbia and Alberta, the western Arctic, the high mountains of Oregon and south to New Mexico. Also in central and northern Europe and Asia.

Arctic Willow
Salix arctica

SALICACEAE

One of the most northern of the willows, this decumbent trailing tree or shrub is circumpolar and occurs in the mountains as well as on the tundra. It grows best in moist situations.

Most willows have been used since about 60 A.D. for their pain-relieving properties. Fresh willow bark contains salicin which was used specifically for fevers by many tribes of North American Indians. Salicin was listed in the u.s. *Pharmacopoeia* from 1882 to 1926. It has since been replaced by synthetic preparations such as aspirin.

This plant hybridizes freely with other dwarf species. It forms mats, grows from two to six inches high, and has woolly leaves from which the hairs disappear as the leaves mature.

Blooms from June to August in the eastern Canadian Arctic, south to Newfoundland and west to the Rocky Mountains and the Selkirks in British Columbia.

Bearberry, Kinnikinick
Arctostaphylos uva-ursi

ERICACEAE

The bearberry's clusters of urn-shaped white or pink flowers nestle among dark, leathery leaves in spring, to be succeeded by brilliant red berries later in the season. This prostrate, trailing evergreen shrub, which often spreads its mats over a wide area in the wild, is a prized ground cover plant for many gardeners, even though it is difficult to transplant. It is a dwarf relative of the beautiful manzanitas of the west.

Both the generic name, *Arctostaphylos*, and the specific name, *uva-ursi*, mean bears' grapes. A common plant throughout the northern parts of the world, it has long been associated, as both the scientific and common names suggest, with food for bears and other animals. In North America it is regularly browsed by deer and the berries eaten by grouse. The second common name, *kinnikinick*, is of Indian origin and indicates that the leaves have been used for smoking.

Blooms from May to July in sandy and rocky areas, on exposed barrens from Labrador to Alaska and south to Virginia, Indiana, northern Illinois, Minnesota, New Mexico and California; also Eurasia.

Mountain Phacelia, Scorpionweed, Silky Phacelia
Phacelia sericea

HYDROPHYLLACEAE

The graceful fernlike leaves are described by the species name as silky, and they feel soft and pliant due to their hairiness. The purple flower cluster is accented by the orange anthers held out on long purple filaments. This lovely perennial adds beauty to Alpine and sub-Alpine slopes.

Phacelia is from the Greek word, *phakelos*, meaning cluster, which describes the arrangement of the flowers. The plant attains a height of six to eighteen inches. There are many species in this genus, all belonging to North or South America.

Blooms from June to August in the mountains of Alberta and British Columbia, south to California and New Mexico.

Cotton Grass, Hare's Tail
Eriophorum spissum

CYPERACEAE

The waving white plumes of the cotton grass ornament the cold, green sphagnum bogs of the north. Really a sedge, as its triangular stem betokens, its minute, brown-green flowers are scarcely noticeable, but the silky, white bristles that develop around the ovary and elongate with the maturing fruit are lovely. There are several related species of cotton grass, not easily told apart, but this is one of the commoner members of the group. It forms tussocks of erect-stemmed plants, each stem being topped by a solitary spikelet of flowers and bristles.

The generic name, *Eriophorum*, means cotton- or wool-bearing. The specific name, *spissum*, means crowded.

Blooms April to July, the 'cotton' being most evident in June and July, in sphagnum bogs, wet meadows and swamps from Baffin Island and Labrador to Alaska, south to New Jersey, N. Indiana, Minnesota and Alberta.

Moss Campion, Moss Pink
Silene acaulis

CARYOPHYLLACEAE

The tiny pink flowers of this plant may completely cover its cushion-like hummocks that cling to the high Alpine rocks. It is mostly found above timberline in stony places. Circumpolar in habitat, one can find it growing in the Alps and the mountains of northern Europe.

Silene is from the Greek god, Silenus, and refers to the stickiness of some species of this genus, for Silenus was described as covered with foam. *Acaulis* means stemless, and describes the way in which the branches grow directly from the root.

It is a real delight to come upon a flowering cushion of moss pink, at a high spot in the mountains. It seems to enjoy the rocky places where few other plants can survive due, no doubt, to its strong deep roots and habit of hugging the rock so that the ice and snow cannot easily tear it away. Protect it that it may gladden other eyes.

Blooms in July and August from Newfoundland to Alaska and south in the mountains to New Hampshire in the east and Montana and Washington in the west.

Shooting Star
Dodecatheon hendersonii

PRIMULACEAE

One of the delights of springtime is to find a group of shooting stars wherever they may bloom. There are many species in this genus whose name was derived from two Greek words, *dodeca*, meaning twelve, and *theos*, god. It is suggested that these lovely flowers are under the care of the twelve superior gods of Greece, but this is of doubtful significance for an American genus.

The flower was named after Professor Louis Henderson, a professor of botany in Oregon. The leaves are said to be edible, but should not be picked, as they will destroy the plant. The flower stem grows to a height of five to eighteen inches.

Blooms May to July in woods and clearings at moderate to low altitudes from British Columbia to California on the Pacific coast.

Baked-apple Berry, Cloudberry
Rubus chamaemorus

ROSACEAE

Like a string of wide-spaced, little white roses, atop a three- to ten-inch shoot, this large-flowered member of the raspberry group reaches out on long runners across moor and bog. Its flowers are succeeded by large, juicy berries that are first red then a beautiful amber in colour.

The generic name, *Rubus*, is an old Roman name, meaning red, and *chamaemorus* means ground mulberry. The plant got its name of baked-apple berry because of its fancied resemblance to a mound of miniature well-baked apples. The other name of cloudberry refers to the association of this plant with cloudy mountains and moors. The fruit, which has a delicate flavour, is highly prized, both as fresh fruit and preserved.

Blooms from June to early August in acid, peaty soils on moors, mountains, rocky shores and bogs from Greenland and Labrador to Alaska, south to Newfoundland, Nova Scotia, the mountains of Maine and New Hampshire; Montauk Point, L.I.; Manitoba, Alberta and British Columbia. Also Eurasia.

Harebell
Campanula rotundifolia

CAMPANULACEAE

The harebell with its tender, bell-shaped blooms displayed upon hairlike stems and bending before every breeze is seemingly the very essence of fragility. None the less, it is one of the most durable and resilient of plants. It may be seen dotting a comfortable lowland meadow, well beyond the timberline in the high mountains or along a storm-wracked Arctic shore; it may cling to a precarious perch on a steep cliff far above a rushing stream or be found under the spray of waterfalls. It is, in fact, a most adaptable plant. Called round-leaved (*rotundifolia*) for the roundish leaves at its base, which commonly disappear by the time of blooming, its stem leaves are long, narrow and pointed. The bells swing in the air from four to twenty inches above the ground on branching stems.

This is the famous bluebell of Scotland, so beloved by poets like Sir Walter Scott and renowned the world around. It is a favourite flower of bumblebees.

Blooms from June to September on rocky banks, shores, meadows, in open woods from Labrador to Alaska and south to Pennsylvania, West Virginia, Illinois, Nebraska, Texas and California; also Eurasia.

Lapland Rosebay
Rhododendron lapponicum

ERICACEAE

In the seemingly empty rocky barrens of Alpine heights or Arctic plains the clustered pink-magenta blooms, each a half-inch or more across, of the Lapland rosebay come as a startling and delightful surprise. Resting among matted, evergreen leaves in some sheltered nook or lee, the flowers, open and cup-shaped, are manifestly those of a true rhododendron. In this species the shrubs, which are covered with rusty scales or dots, are dwarfed, growing only from a few inches to a foot above the ground in their bleak northern homes, where they represent the remarkable adaptability and endurance of the rhododendron genus.

Normally an early spring flower, it persists in a few places, usually maritime, until late summer. Blooms June to September from Greenland to Alaska, south to Newfoundland, the higher mountains of Gaspé, New England and New York, northern British Columbia; Eurasia, circumpolar.

Diapensia
Diapensia lapponica

DIAPENSIACEAE

The bright green, earth-hugging cushions of the diapensia are easily noted in their bare, rocky habitats. When topped by masses of creamy-white, yellow-centred blooms in early spring they are most conspicuous. The flowers, on short, leafless stalks, make their effect by mass. The small leaves are numerous, leathery and densely crowded on the stems, creating terminal rosettes.

This circumpolar northerner, of a small, distinctive family, is related to the interesting pyxie moss of the New Jersey sand barrens and to the much prized galax of the southern Appalachians.

Blooms June and July on open, rocky barrens from Greenland to Alaska, south to the Alpine regions of Quebec, northern New England and New York; Eurasia.

Bear-grass
Xerophyllum tenax

LILIACEAE

Sometimes in solitary grandeur, sometimes like a frothy white stream rushing down a mountainside, the bear-grass is one of the most magnificent of our native lilies. Blooming only once every five to seven years, it raises its noble flowering heads two to six feet in the air. Its common name derives from the tuft of long, grasslike leaves that cluster at its base. At a distance it looks like one great flower but in fact the flowering head is composed of many small blooms, each about half an inch across. In mountain meadows it dominates all its floral neighbours.

The generic name, *Xerophyllum*, means dry leaves, while the specific name of *tenax* adds the qualification of tough or tenacious. Elk and other animals find the flowers, stalks and seed pods excellent fare; in winter mountain goats browse on the tufted leaves and in the spring bears eat the succulent leaf bases. When dried and bleached the leaves were used by Indians for making baskets and for weaving clothing. They also roasted the roots which formed a satisfying food.

Blooms from June to September in open woods and Alpine meadows and on mountain slopes from Alberta to British Columbia, south to Wyoming and California.

Globe Flower
Trollius laxus

RANUNCULACEAE

As soon as the snow melts in the mountain meadows, this hardy flower blooms along streams and in wet places, in great numbers. There are two varieties, one with greenish-yellow flowers and one with white flowers. These flowers have no petals, but the petal-like sepals take their place and surround the striking golden centre of stamens and pistil. It reaches a height of six to twelve inches.

The genus name was taken from a German word *trollblume*, which was the common name of the round yellow globe flower or butterball of Europe, *T. europaeus*. It is a close relative of our globe flower, and is often found as a garden flower. *Laxus* means loose and refers to the way in which it grows.

Blooms from June to August in the mountains of Alberta and British Columbia, and south to Washington and Colorado.

White Mountain Avens
Dryas octopetala

ROSACEAE

The mountain avens is a sun-loving evergreen plant of rock ledges, slopes and rocky stream edges of circumpolar habitat. Although there are several varieties of the species, all have cream or white flowers. The only visible differences are in the edges of the leaves; some are more crenate than others. These species are *D. octopetala*, *D. integrifolia*, *D. hookeriana* and *D. punctata*.

Dryas, the generic name, comes from dryad, the mythological name for a wood nymph, thus calling attention to the resemblance of the tiny leaves to the leaves of some oaks. *Octopetala* refers to the usual eight petals.

The Northwest Territories chose the white mountain avens for their emblem several years ago. The same species can be seen in Switzerland, and across Northern Europe. The conspicuous seed heads are much taller than the flowers, which grow to about five inches.

Blooms in June and July in the high Alpine and Arctic regions of North America, from Newfoundland to Alaska.

Western Anemone, Chalice Flower
Anemone occidentalis

RANUNCULACEAE

The winds of spring blow across thousands of these cup-shaped flowers in the meadows of the mountains of western North America. After blooming, the mops of seeds, called 'towhead babies,' are conspicuous in the mountains. In the fall winds, the seeds, supported by their feathery tails, are blown far and wide, and justify the other common name of wind flower. The flower grows to a height of ten inches, while the seed head reaches fifteen inches.

The Indians of the west probably used one of the species of anemones to stop nosebleed and to treat boils and burns. It is related to the pasque flower, *Anemone patens*, which the Indians also used.

Blooms from May to July in Alberta and British Columbia and southwards, in the western mountains of the United States.

Fields, meadows and other open places

Fields and open spaces abound across this country. Sometimes they are mere pocket openings, forest bound; sometimes miles of geometrical checkerboard fields stretch to the horizon. Even in the mountains fields and open spaces are to be found, both in the valleys and along the slopes. Such areas are scattered everywhere across southern Canada and the northern United States. Some are natural, the products of dryness, drought and wind, of fire and flood; some are made by man, for wherever settlers have gone fields and clearings have been sure to appear. Their existence from one side of the country to the other is tangible proof that this is a settled land.

The characteristics of these fields, meadows and open spaces change from one region to another, thanks to differences of climate, soil, habitat and length of settlement. The distinctions are reflected in all forms of life, not least amongst the plants. When spring comes to the land, the meadows of the Maritimes and Ontario respond with drifts of golden buttercups, while in the Prairies the first noticeable response may be the smoky-blue prairie crocus, or pasque flower. In the intermontane desert flats of southern British Columbia appear the spectacular blooms of the bitteroot, arising often leafless from bare earth, while nearer the coast blue camas cover the meadows. None the less, distinctiveness is only part of the picture, for right across the country, wherever man has gone, there are plants that have travelled with him and which are still on the move. The dandelion flourishes from Atlantic to Pacific, the blue blooms of the chicory cross the land, and the bold black-eyed Susan greets us along roadsides almost everywhere. Such plants give the fields of Canada a common factor. Thus we find that in the fields and open spaces there is a blend of local difference and a common overall presence.

When deciduous woods accompany fields, the first blooms of spring come in the woods, where plants take advantage of the unhampered sunlight which later in the season will be severely cut down by the shadowing leaves. The field flowers of the same area on the other hand will reach their time of greatest variety and abundance during the late spring and the hot days of summer. Their glory, may, indeed, extend even to the first frosts of autumn.

One of the earliest spring flowers, the coltsfoot, raises its yellow blossoms along the damper edges of fields and roadsides shortly after the snow has gone. Soon thereafter the roads become edged with gold, a gold that streams in rivers across field and meadow, the gold of the dandelion, the buttercup and the mustard. Yet, only when sweeps of white ox-eye daisies seem to blow new snow across the fields, when they are joined by pink and white mallow and dozens of associate blooms, may the field flowers be said to have attained their true glory.

On western mountain slopes and in their vales the heyday of bloom in the open spaces also comes in late spring and summer. Then is the time when the scarlet gilia fires its red rockets along bare rocky hills and in flowery valley fields. Then the Indian paintbrush marshals its red battalions across mountain meadow and river flat, accompanied here and there by others of its kind in dress of yellow and cream. On many a mountainside may be seen the great splashes of blue and purple and white of the penstemon, and blue lupines etched against the mountain skyline. Nearly everywhere in these summer months the open spaces present a rich mosaic of bloom.

Greatest of all the open spaces are the grassland prairies which occupy the central part of the continent from the deciduous and mixed forests of the east to the Rocky Mountains in west and which in Canada reach northward to the coniferous forest. This is a natural grassy area and before farms and ranches came to occupy so much of the region, three great bands of distinctive grasses occupied it all. In the eastern and more moist part the bluestem grasses raised their plumed heads four to six feet and even higher in the tall grass prairie. On the dry plains closer to the mountains, where once the great buffalo herds roamed, the short grasses like blue grama and buffalo grass formed a sea of green a few inches high. In between was a band of mixed grasses. The boundaries were not precise but wavered back and forth as climate dictated. The prairies and their natural divisions still exist, though vastly modified, in many places to the point of obliteration, by human occupation in the form of agriculture and grazing.

Although grasses are the predominant plants of the

prairies, associated with the grasses is a varied company of other plants. In this company spring may be ushered in by the blue-grey blooms of the prairie crocus but it will not be long before the fiery prairie or wood lily spangles the meadows alongside prairie roads. Most striking, too are the many locoweeds; they come in many hues, one of the most attractive being the early yellow locoweed. Near at hand one is likely to find milk vetches and many other members of the pea family, including those fanciful prairie clovers whose flowering heads so often make one think of little Victorian hats. The aster family is also much in evidence on the prairies, beginning with the rag-worts and gaillardias in the spring, rising to a climax with the numerous showy sunflowers of the prairie summer, closing the flowering season with the purple, white and gold of aster and goldenrod. Then when all blooms have ceased for the year and frost is in the air we may see the Russian thistle, a plant that came with man to live on the prairies, break loose from its moorings and roll across the field to pile up in tremendous windrows against prairie fences along with tangled masses of other tumbleweeds.

Long stretches of sand—dunes, beaches and barrens— would not at first sight seem to offer much to the flower seeker. Nevertheless, a limited but very interesting group of plants have adapted to such habitats. On beaches, for instance, on both sides of the continent as well as along the shores of the Great Lakes, the silverweed, one of the loveliest of the cinquefoils, sends out its silver-leaved run-ners set with tiny yellow blooms. Equally tenacious is the richly bedecked beach pea whose purple-tinted flowers and mats of green foliage successfully defy both loose sand and scouring winds.

In many parts of the country, sand dunes and hills still travel across the land or stand fixed in sculptured ridges under the grasp of retaining vegetation. These are mute reminders of seas and lakes now long since gone. As the Great Lakes, for example, have withdrawn from their once far greater extent they have left behind, notably along windward shores, miles of dunes, now mostly over-grown. On these dunes grow some very special flowers, such as the lake or dwarf iris. Only inches high this little iris often spreads its blue blooms in such unbroken sheets that it resembles the blue pools of the onetime lake. Up on the more open dunes appear the cream and green flowers of the wide-branching white camas.

Nowhere is the attraction of ancient dunes more appa-rent than in the Spruce Woods Forest Preserve near Bran-don, Manitoba. Here for miles and miles the rising and falling dunes compose the landscape scene, some green with spruce, some fringed with grass, others so naked with sliding sand that one expects to see water lapping at their feet. On these mounds and in these hollows some of the most striking of the prairie flowers find themselves very much at home. Here are found the graceful pink or white umbels of the prairie onion and its cousin, the nod-ding onion, the gold and purple heads of the gaillardia, and the tall hats of the long-headed coneflower, the humorist of the dunes.

It is seldom realized that the northern tip of the great North American desert, which extends north from Mexico through the inner montane area of the United States, stretches into Canada. Those who think of the desert as belonging to states like Arizona, Nevada and Utah are not aware that similar conditions prevail throughout southernmost Saskatchewan, Alberta and British Columbia. Arid but covered with sparse vegeta-tion, the desert bears a flora all its own. No plant is a better indicator of the presence of the desert than the aromatic sagebrush, whose grey clumps set a sombre haze over the land. In British Columbia hundreds of thousands of acres are marked with the sagebrush brand. In the dry desert flats the showy blooms of the bitterroot adorn an otherwise naked space. Nor is any flower more appealing than the lavender cups of the mariposa lily whose deli-cacy and grace seem unbelievable on some sun-scorched slope or plain. Fully believable and very much in place are the thick spiny leaves of the prickly pear cactus, whose brilliant yellow and orange blooms sit so securely beneath the desert sky that they seem to be saying, 'We are equal to the worst that you can produce'. Indeed, the toughness and resilience of desert plants are worthy of everyone's admiration.

Potentially one of the richest and most accessible places to see field and open space flowers are the roadsides of the country. We say, 'potentially', because in so many parts the unhappy practice of road spraying has eliminated all but a bland monochrome of green grass, or has left behind a legacy of ugly, distorted, dead and dying plants, brown, bleak and sad. Much of the spraying would seem to be unnecessary, even to protect overhead wires or to provide clear road vision. Realization of this has brought amelioration of the practice in some places and it is to be hoped that further experience will teach us that we are not required to desolate our surroundings to the extent that we now do. On some main highways and especially along many rural roads the traveller will still find treasuries of bloom. There are roadsides in Nova Scotia where green banks are tinted pink and white with trailing arbutus, where gorse bushes stand like yellow torches beside the road, where multicoloured lupines march in thousands mile after mile. In many parts of Ontario the roadsides are lined with buttercups in spring and a proud parade of purple asters and goldenrods in late summer and fall. Across the prairies sunflowers and coneflowers add grace to roadside views, and in British Columbia there are spots where the pink salmonberry and the white thimbleberry turn roadsides into gardens. In truth, local field plants everywhere could turn most roadsides into gardens if they were only given the chance. A further example of this possibility may be seen along the railroad and its embankments, which frequently provide not only invitations to the plants that travel with man but a space for survivors among our native plants that might otherwise perish in an intensely cultivated land.

Then there are the abandoned and neglected fields, dumps and landfills, waste places and disturbed ground in general. In such areas man has broken up the natural balance and upset natural development. Should he really abandon these places for long, nature will restore the balance in its own way. The proof of this lies in the fact that none of these areas remain bathan a very short time. As they stand they are open opportunities, beckoning invitations to all travelling plants. And all plants can travel, some very slowly and in a limited way, some quickly and over great distances. Anyone who has seen seed-laden milkweed parachutes blowing across autumn fields, or willow fluff whitening the ground in spring, or ample keys sailing through the air knows how some plants travel. He who has picked seed-bearing burs from his dog or off his own clothes has discovered another mode of plant mobility. Remember, too, that quite recently, in geological terms virtually all Canada and most of the northern United States were covered with ice, which on its retreat left behind nothing but bare ground. Almost all that vast area has now been reoccupied by plants that travelled up from the south of their own accord and with the help of wind and water, birds and other animals. They are still travelling and the northward push is still going on.

There are other plants that travel with or in the wake of man, aided and abetted by much that he does. Like domestic animals, they have been long associated with man and they tend to follow wherever he may go. It is to plants of this sort that man's waste places and disturbed grounds offer a special opportunity. The native plant cover having been destroyed or upset, the door is open to newcomers, strangers and immigrants. Sometimes these plants are brought by man as vegetables, fruits or garden ornaments. One good example is the dandelion, introduced by colonists from Europe as a salad green, it 'escaped' to sweep across the land. Another is the tawny hawkweed or devil's paintbrush which was brought to North America just about a hundred years ago as a garden flower. In that short time it has spread so successfully that it now carpets old fields by the acre with its rich orange blooms from the Atlantic to the Great Lakes. Sometimes such plants come unbidden, travelling as seeds in imported grain, caught in the packing about countless goods, embedded in the mud of tourists' cars and in a myriad other ways. All of these are introduced plants which, when established and able to persist on their own, are called naturalized. In some places they make up as much as one-quarter to one-third of the plant population. Mostly they are well known, so well known, and unwanted in fact, that many of them are called weeds. Man does not always like the plants that follow in his path. Still, in the waste places where they so frequently dwell, what seeker after flowers will discount the blue beauty of the chicory, the immaculate white grace of Queen Anne's lace, the bold yellow heads of elecampane and the mellow gold of butter and eggs, all of which belong to this group of plants? In a country where all people are historically settlers come from abroad, it ill behoves any of us to look down upon the introduced and the naturalized. It is far better to see in them the beauty that is rightfully theirs and to enjoy the beautiful weeds that clothe the waste places of our land.

Butter and Eggs, Toadflax
Linaria vulgaris

SCROPHULARIACEAE

Anyone who has looked at an orange egg yolk resting upon well-buttered toast should not be at all surprised at why this flower is called butter and eggs. With its striking blossoms clustered at the top of stems that may rise one, two or three feet high, this handsome plant strongly resembles its cousin, the snapdragon of the gardens, and has itself been frequently used as an ornamental plant. Though disliked by the farmer as a pervasive weed in grainfields and pastures, its gay golden masses on roadside banks are admired by travellers as one of the colourful rewards of summertime trips. The generic name, *Linaria,* refers to the similarity of the leaves to flax (*linum*).

In former days an infusion was made from the leaves and used in various medicinal ways. For example, its juice, mixed with milk, was employed as a fly poison. And from the flowers a good yellow dye was made.

Blooms from May to October in fields, pastures, roadsides and waste places across Canada and the United States. Also in Eurasia.

Canada Goldenrod
Solidago canadensis

COMPOSITAE

As summer wanes, nothing is more striking than the carpets of gold that clothe the fields, spreading along unsprayed roadside banks and marking the edges of woodland trails. These are all different goldenrods, members of that basically North American genus that reaches its greatest variety in the eastern United States. Of all the many species the one pictured here, Canada goldenrod, is one of the commonest. It has plume-like floral branches with massed clusters of small golden flower heads which tend to be ranked on one side of the branch. The narrow, well-toothed leaves are sharply pointed, and the plants grow from one to five feet tall. The generic name, *Solidago*, means to make whole and refers to the once-supposed curative and healing qualities of the genus.

Though unappreciated in America by gardeners, no doubt because it is so common, and condemned by farmers as a pestiferous weed, it is regarded in England, France and other European countries as a valuable garden flower and has long been cultivated there. In the valley of the Loire it has gone wild. The flowers of the goldenrod have been used to make a yellow dye and the Indians made medicinal brews of both flowers and roots.

Blooms from mid-July to September, occasionally later, in fields, roadsides and open woods from Newfoundland to Saskatchewan, south to North Carolina, Tennessee, South Dakota and Colorado.

Common Nightshade
Solanum dulcamara

SOLANACEAE

Sometimes called bittersweet (which confuses this with the completely different American bittersweet) these berries are found on a common weed. The flowers are pale purple with strongly reflexed petals and a protruding pistil partially surrounded by bright yellow stamens. The plant is a climbing vine, three to six feet long. It was introduced from Europe, and it grows in clearings and near to settlements. It is a weed in many gardens.

These berries are poisonous; they contain solanine, which is also present in the berries of the black nightshade, *S. nigrum,* and in the similar black fruits of *S. belladonna.* Solanine is violently toxic when eaten in quantity, causing injury to the digestive organs and later affecting the nervous system. Cattle eating the plants have died and children should be warned against them. They are said to taste bitter when chewed, and then sweet, hence the species name *dulcamara,* and the common one, bittersweet.

Blooms from May to September (fruit: from July to October), throughout eastern North America, and occasionally in the west.

Indian Thistle
Cirsium edule

COMPOSITAE

The Greek word, *kirsos*, was used to create the generic name. It means a swollen vein, and thistles were believed to cure this condition. *Edule* refers to the edibility of this species. The parts eaten were the peeled roots and stem. Thistles are easily recognized by their large flowers and prickly leaves and stem, except in one or two species. There are about two hundred species in North America.

The edible Indian thistle is distinctive because of the cobwebby hairs on the bracts below the flowers. This feature is shown in the picture. It grows to a height of four to seven feet.

Thistles are a good survival food since they grow over most of North America. Peeling the stems or roots is one way to get rid of the spines. The inner parts can be boiled. The down of the thistle seeds is helpful in starting a fire when matches are not available, as it catches fire easily from a spark.

Blooms from April to September on the west coast of North America, from British Columbia to Washington.

Tall White Lettuce, Rattlesnake Root
Prenanthes altissima

COMPOSITAE

So tall (up to seven feet or more) that children sometimes measure their height against it, this tallest of the white lettuces hangs its creamy-white funnel-shaped blooms in graceful axillary or terminal clusters. Its thin, broad, usually coarse-toothed leaves can be very variable in shape; being sometimes triangular, lobed or entire, arrow or heart-shaped near the bottom of the plant, progressively smaller and simpler towards the top. The shorter but very similar *P. alba* differs only slightly in details of flower pattern. The generic name, *Prenanthus*, means drooping flower, while *altissima* describes this species as being very tall.

Once thought to be a remedy for snakebite, it received the common name of rattlesnake root. Its bitter roots have also been used in herbal medicine as a tonic.

Blooms July to October at the edge of or in damp woods from Nova Scotia, Quebec and Manitoba south to Georgia, Tennessee and Louisiana.

Field Chickweed, Starry Chickweed
Cerastium arvense

CARYOPHYLLACEAE

Starry aptly describes this charming little flower, one of the many beautiful weeds of dry fields, sandy or rocky places. It grows from sea level to Alpine height, preferring calcareous soils. The stems are six to fifteen inches tall, but may be partially on the ground. Its five deeply cleft petals are characteristic of the pink family.

Cerastium is from the Greek *cerastes*, meaning horned, which alludes to the shape of the seed capsule. *Arvense* means field, thus its common name.

Chickweeds are edible, raw or cooked. The closely related common chickweed, *Stellaria media*, is a very widespread weed, and in all our gardens. It is more highly recommended as a herb and is said to taste like spinach. Next time you are pulling it out of your garden, try it!

Blooms from April in southern lowlands to August in high and northern habitats, from Greenland to Alaska and south throughout Canada and the United States; also Eurasia.

Birdfoot Violet
Viola pedata

VIOLACEAE

This is the most beautiful of the violets of eastern North America. This large-flowered plant is more common in the south. Along the shore of Lake Erie in Ontario, it is rare and needs protection.

The flowers may be all one colour, usually lilac-purple, or bi-coloured, the upper two petals dark violet and the lower three, lilac-coloured. *Viola* is the classical name for this cosmopolitan genus, and *pedata* means like a foot. Its distinctive deeply cleft leaves do resemble a spread-open bird's foot. These leaves are very variable, and there are several other species with similar leaves but without such large beardless flowers. The usual height is four to six inches.

Both flower and leaf stalks grow directly from the rhizome (root) which is characteristic of the stemless violets. Our many kinds of garden pansies were developed from a wild violet of Europe, *Viola tricolor.* As can be seen in all violets, the lower centre petal of the five is spurred in the pansies.

Blooms from April to June, in Ontario, and south from Maine to Minnesota, and down to Kansas, Florida and Texas.

Ox-eye Daisy, Marguerite
Chrysanthemum leucanthemum

COMPOSITAE

So common as to be taken for granted, the ox-eye daisy did not exist in North America before the English and French colonists brought it out to their gardens as a memento of homelands far away. Long ago escaped and now naturalized from coast to coast, in spring its blooms scatter with snowy white the roadbanks, fields and pastures. If daisies give a queer taste to cow's milk, they have also made sport for young lovers to play the game, 'She loves me, she loves me not.' To horticulturists and geneticists they give endless opportunities for experimentation; for example, Luther Burbank's Shasta daisy had this plant as one of its ancestors.

Blooms May to October in fields and roadsides from Labrador to British Columbia, south to Florida, Texas and California.

Pokeweed Berries
Phytolacca americana

PHYTOLACCACEAE

On dusty roadsides, on dry fields and disturbed ground throughout eastern North America, this tall red stemmed plant may be seen. It is especially noticeable in late summer and fall when its inconspicuous pink or white flowers have turned into shiny purple black berries. These heavy clusters weigh down the ends of the red stems. The plant may grow as high as ten feet, but dies back in winter. Its huge root is difficult to dig up, and may be six inches thick.

The plant is poisonous in all parts, but the berries and the large taproot are most dangerous. Cattle have died from eating too many fresh young shoots, and humans from eating too many berries. Indians and early settlers made a purgative medicine from the root, but overdoses of this infusion have been known to be fatal. However, the very young shoots when boiled in several waters can be used as a vegetable.

The name comes from the Greek word *phyton* for plant, and the Latin, *lacca*, meaning crimson. The berries yield a dark red dye, formerly used as an ink which had long-lasting qualities. Birds of many species are said to feed on the berries with impunity. Its other common English names are ink-berry, red ink plant, pigeon berry, scoke, and Virginia poke.

Blooms July to October from Ontario to Quebec and south to Florida and Texas.

Orange Hawkweed, Devil's Paintbrush
Hieracium aurantiacum

COMPOSITAE

A familiar weed in fields and along roadsides, it is a perennial with running roots as well as wind-born seeds. It often grows to a height of two feet, and spreads rapidly wherever it grows. An immigrant from Europe, it has invaded many fields and ruined good pasture-land. The farmers named it devil's paint-brush. Not eaten by cattle because of its hairi-ness, it has displaced more useful plants.

The species name, *aurantiacum*, means orange, the colour of the flower. The generic name came from the Greek word, *hierax*, meaning a hawk, hence the English name. The Roman historian, Pliny, wrote that hawks ate the plant to strengthen their eyesight. Thus, long ago, herb doctors made eye lotions from it.

Blooms from June to August from Min-nesota to Newfoundland, south to Virginia; also on the Pacific coast.

Teasel
Dipsacus sylvestris
DIPSACEAE

The lilac-banded, egg-like flowering heads of the teasel are tempting to the would-be picker. But contact with the many stout spines on stem, leaves and flower heads themselves, soon convinces him to leave them alone. This biennial, that produces rosettes of crinkly green leaves one year and sends up flowering stalks two to seven feet high the next, is one of the most striking late summer plants of our fields. The small, lilac-coloured, tubular flowers packed on the oval head start to bloom in the middle of the head as a rule and work up and down its length. The generic name, *Dipsacus*, is said to mean thirst and to refer to the fact that the leaves, cupped at the stem, often hold water, so might relieve thirst. The specific name, *sylvestris* means of the woods and is a misnomer as this plant grows in the open.

Brought originally from Europe, it resembles a close relative (*D. fullonum*), which was used to tease up the nap from the cloth (the dried heads being placed upon revolving spindles for the purpose), hence the common name of teasel. Nowadays the dried heads are frequently used in winter bouquets, either plain or painted. Many farmers regard teasel as an obnoxious weed.

Blooms July to October in old fields, waste land, roadsides and similar places from Quebec to Michigan, south to North Carolina and Tennessee, west to Utah; on the Pacific coast from British Columbia south to California.

Common Milkweed
Asclepias syriaca
ASCLEPIADACEAE

The common milkweed blooms in rounded clusters of pink or lavender. The flowers arc or hang semi-pendant in the axils of tall, broad-leaved plants that may rise up to six feet or more. The blooms are hooded and horned in the manner of the family while the warty, grey-green pods open to reveal masses of silvery-plumed seeds that are characteristic of this species. Occasionally the flowers are yellow or white. It is an aggressive plant and may grow in tremendous colonies.

The seed pods are a boon to the makers of dry bouquets, while the young shoots have been prized as a substitute for asparagus. Experiments to extract rubber from the milky juice and to use the silky fluff as a textile or packing have been tried without much success. It is very attractive to insects, which sometimes die by becoming entangled in the flowers.

Blooms June to August in fields and roadsides from New Brunswick to Saskatchewan, south to Georgia, Tennessee and Kansas.

Pale Corydalis
Corydalis sempervirens

FUMARIACEAE

Korydalis is the Greek name for the crested lark. Because this flower has a small spur on its top petal and a fancied resemblance to a bird, it was named for it. *Sempervirens* means evergreen. The leaves develop in late fall and may winter over in some climates.

The pink and yellow flowers appear in early summer. They are small and look fragile, and the leaves are fernlike and blue-green. The plant reaches a height of two feet.

Blooms May to September in rocky places and open dry woods, Newfoundland to Alaska, south to British Columbia, and Montana, and in the mountains of the east to Georgia.

Three-flowered Avens, Prairie Smoke
Geum triflorum

ROSACEAE

Blooming early, the three-flowered avens first tints the prairies pink; when the feathery seed heads ripen, it creates the illusion of smoke floating across the prairies, as the tall plumes wave in the breeze. The plant grows to a height of six to eighteen inches. The flowers are pale pink or flesh-coloured. The petals are almost hidden by the deep pink sepals. Three flowers grow on one stem, hence *triflorum*. Geum is the early Latin name used for this genus by Pliny. There are several other species of geum in North America.

Blooms from April to July in dry fields and prairies, from Ontario to British Columbia and southwest to California.

Evening Primrose
Oenothera biennis

ONAGRACEAE

Sturdy, growing up to six feet, and crowned with spikes of showy yellow flowers, the evening primrose is one of the best-known plants of our summer fields and roadsides. Like other members of the genus, of which there are many species on this continent, these flowers have a quite distinctive cross-shaped stigma. The stems are hairy and often reddish. When the flowers give way to spikes of long, green pods, one of nature's most striking patterns is created. As a biennial it sets rosettes of prominent light-green leaves that winter over and send up the next year's flowering stalks.

So variable is this species, indeed the whole genus, that it provided Hugo de Vries, a century ago, with the bulk of the material for the working out of his theory of evolution by mutation.

Blooms June to October from Newfoundland to British Columbia, south to Florida, Texas and Arizona.

Starry False Solomon's Seal
Smilacina stellata

LILIACEAE

The white star-flowered clusters of the starry false Solomon's seal appear on moist open banks in spring. Their upright stems bear alternate, lance-shaped leaves and may rise to two feet or more tall. The single flowers are larger, fewer and more loosely arranged than those of the crowded, branched heads of its relative, false spikenard (*S. racemosa*). However, this plant is not as small as its bog cousin, the three-leaved false Solomon's seal (*S. trifolia*). Despite its unfortunate common name it bears only a slight resemblance to true Solomon's seal, whose arching leafy stems with bell-like flowers hanging down from the leaf axils have a quite different appearance. The starry flowers produce dramatic berries that are first tan, striped with dark purple, then red and finally almost black. These berries provide food for ruffed grouse, several species of thrush and white-footed mice.

Blooms from May to August in open meadows, bluffs, shores and woods, especially on sandy soil, from Newfoundland to British Columbia, south to New Jersey, West Virginia, Kansas, New Mexico and California.

Wild Columbine
Aquilegia canadensis

RANUNCULACEAE

The blooms of the columbine hang like exquisite little lanterns, scarlet-spurred and with a tiny light shining in each, offset with graceful three-parted leaves. From one to three feet high, the columbine loves rock-strewn areas and often fills them with vibrant colour.

The colourful flowers provide a great attraction to hummingbirds. They are also patronized by long-tongued moths and butterflies. Those insects that cannot get at the nectar in the spurs in the ordinary way are in the habit of taking a short cut by piercing through the point of the spur.

It has been noted that the Indians rubbed columbine on their hands as a love charm, and used the seeds and the roots medicinally. These seeds were so much in demand that they were an article of trade among the tribes.

Blooms from April to July in rocky wooded places, on cliffs and ledges from Newfoundland, Nova Scotia and Quebec to Saskatchewan, south to Florida, Alabama and Texas.

Fireweed, Great Willow Herb
Epilobium angustifolium

ONAGRACEAE

Wherever a forest fire has blackened the landscape, the bright pink of fireweed springs up to cover the scar. It grows very well in disturbed ground, and usually covers the edges of a newly built road, when no sod is laid down. It can be seen in open places creating a patch of colour with its graceful spires which may grow as tall as six feet.

When the long slender seed pods split open, the seeds expand their downy parachutes and sail away on the wind. Underground, the spreading roots produce new plants. It is a very widespread plant; chosen as the emblem of the Yukon, it is common in that territory.

Epilobium is from two Greek words, *epi*, meaning upon and *lobon*, a capsule. This describes the way in which the petals surmount the ovary. *Angustifolium* means narrow-leaved, as opposed to the other common willow herb, *E. latifoliium*, the broad-leaved, which is similar, but not so tall.

Blooms from July to September from the sub-Arctic region south to Arizona and California, and from the east to the west coasts.

Black-eyed Susan
Rudbeckia hirta
COMPOSITAE

In midsummer black-eyed Susans are a common sight on sunny banks and in warm, dry fields. One to three feet tall, the plants sometimes stand alone but are more often found in sociable clusters, enlivening whole stretches of the countryside. They belong to the coneflower group, for in the midst of the conspicuous golden yellow or orange ray flowers is a raised disc of dark brown or purplish florets, whose widening circle of successive bloom makes a ring of yellow when the pollen is ripe. Stems and leaves are both rough and bristly.

This genus was named *Rudbeckia* in honour of two professors, father and son, who were predecessors of the famous Linnaeus at the University of Uppsala in Sweden. The specific name, *hirta,* means rough and describes the general feel of the plant.

Apparently a native of the Great Plains region, the black-eyed Susan has moved both east and west. Most commonly, it would seem, its seed becomes mixed with clover seed shipments, and as a result the plant can now be found from coast to coast. It may also have been native in the Atlantic coast area from Pennsylvania south, as it seems likely that the first specimen named by science in 1732 came from that region. This is the state flower of Maryland.

Blooms from June to October in fields, roadsides, and waste places from Nova Scotia to British Columbia and south to Florida, Texas and California.

Hedge Bindweed
Convolvulus sepium

CONVOLVULACEAE

Pink or white, the large funnel-shaped blossoms of the hedge bindweed reveal their family relationship to the cultivated morning glory. Clambering over roadside thickets, old walls and fences, they add colour and grace to many a neglected corner. The size of the flower, one to two inches, its two broad, leafy bracts and the large leaves set this plant apart from its commoner cousin, the field bindweed (*C. arvensis*), which has much smaller flowers and no floral bracts. Twisting tight shut in the evening, the flower opens early at dawn. The generic name, *Convolvulus,* means to entwine, describing the normal habit of the plant. The specific name, *sepium,* or hedges, refers to its common growth in hedgerows. Some of the many different forms of this plant have been tried in gardens but have been found hard to control. It is regarded as a weed by most farmers.

Blooms May to September in scrubby waste places and roadsides from Newfoundland to British Columbia, south to Florida, Texas, New Mexico and Oregon.

Butterfly Weed
Asclepias tuberosa
ASCLEPIADACEAE

The burnt orange of this lovely milkweed is
one of the richest of nature's colours, attractive to naturalists and butterflies alike. The
brilliant blooms, hooded and horned in the
manner of milkweeds generally, crown plants
that rise two to three feet high on distinctly
hairy stems. Curiously, it lacks the milky
juice of its fellow milkweeds. The long slender pods have the look of elegant brown
suede. The generic name, *Asclepias,* indicates
that the plant is dedicated to the ancient
Greek doctor, Aesclepius.

  The Indians used both the thick rhizomes
(underground stems) and the young seed
pods as food; some even made sugar from the
flowers. Indians and colonists both used this
plant in their folk medicine. It is said to be
poisonous to livestock but they usually leave
it alone.

  Blooms June to September in dry, open,
commonly sandy areas from New Hampshire
to Ontario, Minnesota and Colorado, south
to Florida, Texas and Arizona.

Russian Thistle, Saltwort
Salsola kali

CHENOPODIACEAE

The Latin for salt, *salsus*, is the word from
which the generic name comes, and *kali* is
from the Persian for a large carpet.
Introduced from Europe, it is regarded as a
troublesome weed which is very common on
the prairies. Though edible to cattle, it is very
laxative. It thrives on arid land and in waste
places. When mature the stem breaks off near
the ground, and the plant becomes one of the
tumbleweeds which blow across the prairies,
to pile up against any fence, scattering seeds
as it goes. It is said to taste salty, and to
deserve its other name of saltwort. This shrub
grows up to three feet high.

    Blooms from July to October from Quebec
to British Columbia and south throughout
the United States.

Longheaded Coneflower
Ratibida columnifera

COMPOSITAE

This bright flower can be found in summer on dry prairies and foothills of the midwest. The column-like receptacle on which the true flowers are based (for this is a composite flower) is distinctive, and gives the flower its species and common names.

It grows one to two feet high. Well known on the grasslands of the midwest, it was used by the Indians to produce a yellow-orange dye. The flower heads, when dried, are said to make a palatable tea.

Blooms from June to September from Ontario to British Columbia and south to the prairies of the midwestern United States.

Gumweed
Grindelia integrifolia
COMPOSITAE

These gay daisylike flowers grow along the windswept rocky shores of the Pacific. The sticky buds and bracts of the flower head are distinctive to the several species known in the west. There are fifty species in this genus, of which five are native to western North America. The genus was named in honour of David Grindel (1766–1836) a Russian botanist. The species name means entire-leaved, describing the leaves of the upper stem.

The flowers are held high on a stem growing to one to two and a half feet. This was regarded by the Indians as a useful medicinal plant. A decoction was made from the leaves and applied as a soothing lotion to the irritation caused by poison ivy or poison oak.

Blooms from June to August from southern Alaska to northern California.

Wild Bergamot
Monarda fistulosa

LABIATAE

The open verges of woodland roads, if unsprayed, and abandoned pastures are often ablaze with the purple blooms of the wild bergamot in midsummer. Except in colour, the handsome, rounded heads of long, tubular, two-lipped flowers of this plant are similar to those of its near relative, the scarlet beebalm (*M. didyma*). A circle of pointed, green bracts, that can be pink-hued, set off the flowering heads. The flowers themselves are occasionally pink or white, and the plants grow from three to five feet.

The generic name, *Monarda*, indicates that this plant was dedicated to Nicoles Monardes, a writer on medicinal plants, especially those brought from the New World, in the sixteenth century. The specific name, *fistulosa*, means tubular, and describes the shape of the flowers.

This showy flower was one of the first North American plants to be noted and scientifically named in Europe. Its minty leaves have been widely used for tea, as a flavouring in cooking and as a pot herb. The Indians used it in an aromatic hair pomade.

Blooms June to September in dry clearings, borders of woods and roadsides from Quebec to British Columbia, south to Georgia, Texas, Arizona and Mexico.

Scarlet Gilia
Gilia aggregata
POLEMONIACEAE

The generic name of this handsome flower was given to honour a Spanish botanist, Felipe Luis Gil, by the members of the Spanish expedition to Peru and Chile, where the first plant of this genus was discovered. *Gilia aggregata* was first collected by Lewis and Clarke in California.

The tubular red flowers are favourites with hummingbirds for their nectar. They are clustered at the top of the slender stem, which grows to three feet. Unfortunately this gilia has an unpleasant smell which accounts for its other name, skunk flower.

Blooms from May to August in dry areas from Saskatchewan to British Columbia and throughout the western United States.

Prairie Crocus, Pasque Flower
Anemone patens

RANUNCULACEAE

This brave flower might have been called the harbinger of spring, for it blooms even before the snow has melted from the prairies. As it faces the wind chilled by the melting snow, the hairs on stem, leaves and sepals help to protect it. Coloured from pale to deep mauve, the flowers may be so numerous as to make the prairie look smoky, so it is sometimes called prairie smoke. Its lovely golden stamens contrast well with the sepals.

Named after the Greek word meaning wind, another name is windflower. Pasque flower is also suitable, as the purple sepals were used by early settlers to dye their Easter eggs in the European tradition. In summer the sepals drop off and the feathery seed heads also wave in the wind. The plant contains ranunculin and is potentially dangerous to livestock, though there is no proof of loss. This flower is the floral emblem of the state of South Dakota and of the province of Manitoba.

Blooms in March and April on prairies and on the foothills of the Rockies, from Alaska south to Texas and as far east as Michigan.

Coltsfoot
Tussilago farfara
COMPOSITAE

Native of Eurasia, this immigrant to North America likes disturbed ground, waste places and roadsides. Its name comes from *tussis,* the Latin for cough, for which it was considered a cure. It is believed that settlers from Europe brought the seeds, so that they would have this remedy. The flower stalks were made into a preparation and honey added, as a cough syrup. *Farfarus* is the Latin name for colt's foot, referring to the shape of the leaf.

The flower might be mistaken for a dandelion, as both bloom in early spring. However, the flower of coltsfoot appears before the leaves develop. The late-appearing leaves are large and heart-shaped.

Blooms in March and April from Newfoundland to Minnesota and south to Ohio, Pennsylvania and New Jersey.

Satin Flower, Grass Widows
Sisyrinchium douglasii

IRIDACEAE

The most attractive member of this genus, it was named for David Douglas (1798–1834), the Scottish botanist who collected for the Royal Horticultural Society of England. He probably collected this plant during one of his two trips to the west coast in 1825 and 1830.

The rich rose-red blossoms of this first cousin to the blue-eyed grass bloom in the spring in grassy and rocky places in the west. The flower stems and grasslike leaves may be twelve inches high. The flowers are large, about one and one half inches across.

Blooms from March to June from British Columbia to Nevada and south to California.

Red Clover
Trifolium pratense

LEGUMINOSAE

The Latin name is very descriptive, for
Trifolium means three-leaved, and *pratense*,
of meadows. The leaves are distinctly three-
parted and its favourite habitat is in the
bright sunshine of open places, where it may
grow to a height of sixteen inches. It is the
state flower of Vermont.

It is reported that when red clover was
grown in Australia, as forage, it did not set
seed because there were no bumblebees. The
plant is a native of Europe, but has been
grown extensively in North America for
many years. We have lots of bumblebees, and
red clover has gone wild in our land. The
tongue of the bee is just the right length to
reach the nectary of the flower. While doing
this, the insect catches pollen on its hairs and
carries it to the next flower it visits. So
bumblebees were imported to Australia and
the red clover set seed.

Blooms from May to September in fields
and along roadsides from Labrador to British
Columbia and south throughout the United
States.

Tufted Vetch, Cow Vetch
Vicia cracca
LEGUMINOSAE

The tufted vetch brings such grace and colour to the hedgerows, old fields and roadsides of midsummer that it can be forgiven its reputation as a weed. The compact, one-sided cluster, one to four inches long, bear ten to forty flowers each, all facing downward. They grow on scrambling vines, two to six feet long, whose compound leaves, each with five to fourteen pairs of leaflets, end in a branched tendril with which the plant climbs.

Brought long ago from Europe, where it has been cultivated both as an ornamental and as a fodder plant, it is now completely naturalized in North America, though commonest in the east. This vetch is rich with nectar and much sought by honey bees.

Blooms from May to August (sometimes later) in fields, thickets and roadsides from Newfoundland to British Columbia, south to Virginia and Illinois; Eurasia.

May Apple
Podophyllum peltatum

BERBERIDACEAE

The waxy-white blooms of the May apple, almost two inches across, arching from between the stems of two large, over-shadowing leaves, are among the half-hidden faces of spring. Often growing in tremendous colonies, frequently the plants, one to almost two feet high, do not bear many flowers and seem in consequence like a sheet of polished green, occasionally punctuated by white. Later in the summer will come the shiny, yellow fruit, an inch or more in length, which gives the plant its common name. The generic name, *Podophyllum*, means a leaf with a foot and probably refers to the long petiole (stem) on the basal leaf. The specific name, *peltatum*, means shaped like a shield and refers to the main leaves.

The fruit is bland and sweet and its pulp has been used since colonial days for making jams, jellies and preserves and in beverages. Though other parts of the plant are deemed poisonous, they have been widely used in folk medicine.

Blooms from April to June in rich, open woods, old pastures and meadows, and on shady roadbanks from western Quebec and southern Ontario to Minnesota and south to Florida and Texas.

Purple Clematis, Mountain Clematis
Clematis verticillaris

RANUNCULACEAE

Secretive, elusive, yet as seductive as a siren, the purple clematis hangs its large, satiny bells among shadowed limestone cliffs or along shaded, rocky woodland slopes. Never common, this rarity sets a challenge for every seeker after floral charm and promises a rich reward. The parent vines bear three-parted leaves and set them in pairs along the stem. The flowers are succeeded by feathery mounds of tasseled achenes which, when seen backlit, possess a fascinating silvery sheen. So closely alike are this plant and the famous blue clematis of the Rocky Mountains that the two are included in the same species by some botanists.

Blooms in May and June in rocky woods, often calcareous, from Quebec to Manitoba, south to North Carolina, Ohio and Iowa.

Pink Prairie Clover
Petalostemum purpureum

LEGUMINOSAE

One of the most attractive of all the prairie wildflowers of summer, this clover is a member of the widespread pea family. It may be upright with a height of up to two feet, or it may lie prostrate on the ground. The flowers differ from the usual pea structure in having no keel. All five petals are almost the same size and shape. All the native clovers were used by the dwellers of the prairies as food and fodder.

Blooms from June to September in dry places from Manitoba to Alberta, south to Montana and New Mexico.

Bunchberry
Cornus canadensis

CORNACEAE

The robust white flowers of this dwarf dogwood light up dark evergreen glades, nestle against old fallen trees and brighten the edges of rock faces all across the land. Though it grows well beyond the great conifer forest, it is one of the most characteristic elements of the flora of that vast, dark, northern woodland. The creamy-white 'blooms,' greenish when young, are really prominent sepals. They are a lure for insects, and provide a frame for the tiny, true flowers that are so small as to be easily overlooked. Though growing only two inches to a foot high, the bunchberry has a definite family resemblance to its relatives, the flowering dogwoods, red osier and others.

The common name of bunchberry shows that the brilliant red berries, produced by the tiny flowers, attract more attention than the blooms. To veeries, some vireos and other birds these lovely berries mean food.

Blooms from late May to July, fruiting from late July to October, in damp, acid woods, thickets and upland slopes from southern Greenland and Labrador across Canada to Alaska, south to Maryland, Ohio, Illinois, South Dakota, New Mexico and California. Also northeastern Asia.

Prairie Sunflower
Helianthus petiolaris

COMPOSITAE

To summer travellers along the roads of the high, dry prairies nothing is more characteristic than the smiling yellow faces of the sunflowers seen against the blue of prairie skies. There are about sixty species of sunflowers growing in North America, almost two-thirds of all those in the world. They are scattered across the continent but are at their best on the prairies and in the west. The present species is closely related to the big sunflower that is raised for seed and oil, but it is a much slenderer plant with smaller flowers. It grows anything from about nine inches to nine feet tall, with alternate, wedge-shaped leaves, stems that are hairy near the top and reddish-purple disk flowers at its centre. The specific name, *petiolaris*, shows that the leaves are markedly petioled or 'stemmed'.

Sunflowers in general produce large, nutritious seeds that are much relished by many kinds of seed-eating birds, by many rodents and some deer. This species has travelled eastward, probably chiefly in railway ballast, and is now established in many places there.

Blooms from June to October in dry, open, chiefly sandy places from Manitoba and Minnesota to Washington, south to Louisiana and California. Occasional in the East in areas such as Ontario, New England, New Jersey, Virginia and probably elsewhere.

Prairie Lily, Wood Lily
Lilium philadelphicum

LILIACEAE

Over many years, the species name has been changed. Some time ago, the brilliant red lily of the prairies was called *Lilium montanum*, and sometimes *Lilium andinum*. Now the botanists have decided that there is only one species, and have adopted for all the name *Lilium philadelphicum*, (which formerly designated the paler wood lily of the eastern part of North America). This name was chosen by Linnaeus because the specimen he had was collected near Philadelphia, Pennsylvania.

The orange-to-red lily lifts its cup-shaped flower up above the grass of the prairie or the low growth of open woods. It blooms in early summer from a bulb which was once used as food by the Indians of the Fraser River valley. Dr. Cheadle, who crossed Canada in 1863, writes in his diary that they were 'very bitter and quite spoiled our pemmican stew.' Indians and other travellers considered them a good substitute for potatoes.

In 1941, the prairie lily was officially adopted as the provincial emblem of Saskatchewan. The same flower was used on a five-cent stamp by Canada in 1966.

Blooms June to August in dry or wet woodlands, prairies and openings, Quebec to British Columbia and south as far as New Mexico.

Poison Ivy
Rhus radicans

ANACARDIACEAE

The glossy, dark green leaves of the poison ivy come in threes. Each leaf has three leaflets on a distinct stem, each leaflet being ovate, toothless or sometimes crenate or with a few tooth-like small lobes. The loose clusters of tiny, greenish-white flowers are inconspicuous among the dominant leaves, but the fruit comes in noticeable bunches of whitish berries that stay on from fall to spring. This variable plant may be low and straggling, a sturdy low bush or a thick-stemmed vine clambering over sand dunes and hillsides or high up in tall trees. In the autumn the leaves turn a brilliant red. The specific name of *radicans* means rooting, which this plant does profusely both by aerial roots and by underground runners.

It should always be treated with the utmost care, for the poisonous oil which it contains in all parts of the plant can cause painful and serious skin eruptions. If anyone is evidently affected a doctor should be consulted at once.

Blooms May to July in rocky or sandy open places, woods, roadsides and fence rows, often in tremendous abundance, from Nova Scotia to British Columbia, south to Florida, Texas and Arizona.

Thimbleberry
Rubus parviflorus

ROSACEAE

The generic name for this flower comes from the Latin for red, referring to the colour of the fruit, which is said to be juicy and of a pleasant flavour. *Parviflorus* means small-flowered, which is a misnomer, since the flowers are large, sometimes up to two inches in width.

This almost thornless shrub grows tall, up to six feet high. The fruit is very thin and grows on a large receptacle. When the berry is removed—a delicate operation, so as not to crush the fruit—its shape resembles a small thimble, hence the common name of thimbleberry. The fruit ripens in late summer and was used by the Indians as fruit or made into cakes and dried. It is rich in Vitamin C. The young shoots were eaten as a vegetable.

Blooms from June to September along roadsides and at borders of woods, from Ontario to Alaska and south in the mountains to Arizona and California.

Shrubby St. John's Wort, Kalm's St. John's Wort
Hypericum kalmianum

HYPERICACEAE

Named for St. John the Baptist, because it was in bloom on his birthday, June 24, a legend claims that dew taken from the plant on this day was good as an eye lotion. The species name honours Peter Kalm, the Finnish pupil of Linnaeus who travelled widely in North America in search of plants in 1748. *Hypericum* is taken from two Greek words, *hyper*, meaning above, and *icon*, image. This was an old Greek name for this group of plants.

There are quite a few species of St. John's wort which grow across Canada and the United States. This species is common near the Great Lakes, in rocky or sandy open spaces, and grows to a height of three feet.

Blooms from July to September in Quebec and Ontario, and south to New York, Ohio, Illinois and Indiana.

Common Thistle, Bull Thistle
Cirsium vulgare
COMPOSITAE

Classed as an aggressive weed and armoured from head to foot with a thorny protection that discourages close investigation, the bull thistle hardly seems an attractive flower. None the less, few can avoid a fleeting admiration for the sturdy plant with its brush-like flower heads of pink or magenta standing so boldly beside the road or in the field. Growing from two to six feet high, it may be distinguished from other thistles by its spiny leaf surface and spines along the leaf edges, by its winged stems with long-pointed prickles, and by its rigid, yellow-tipped spines on the flower bracts. The generic name, *Cirsium*, means a swollen vein, for which Dioscorides believed the thistle was a remedy.

This is one of the plants that travels with man and follows him wherever he cultivates farms or creates waste land. As a weed it may be eliminated by careful cultivation. It has a great attraction for butterflies.

Blooms from June to October in pastures, fields, waste places and roadsides from Newfoundland to British Columbia and throughout the United States. A native of Eurasia.

Prickly Pear, Indian Fig
Opuntia polyacantha

CACTACEAE

These lovely fragile flowers are plentiful on
the warm dry hills of the midwest, but can
also be found in the arid interior of British
Columbia and on the Gulf Islands. Archibald
Menzies, the botanist with Captain George
Vancouver, was surprised to find them there
in 1792.

The generic name is derived from Opun-
tium, a town in Greece, but the connection is
obscure, for these plants are native to
America. Christopher Columbus took some
seeds back to Europe and one species has
become common around the Mediterranean
in hot arid rocky places. *Polyacantha* means
with many thorns and is very appropriate.
Beware of these spines as they can pierce a
shoe and go into the foot inside. Early travellers on the prairies complained of three per-
secutors — 'musquitoes, gnats and prickly
pear.' Lewis and Clark, and John Palliser all
wrote of the poisonous penetrating spines.
Even now, skiers who have the bad luck to
fall on a hillside, covered under the snow
with the cacti, have good reason to regret
their choice of landing area.

The leaves of some prickly pears may be
used as an emergency food if they are roasted
in hot ashes and the skin and spines dis-
carded. There are many species in the genus.
The fruit of many kinds is edible.

Blooms May to July from British Columbia
to Manitoba and south to Utah and New
Mexico.

Wild Flax
Linum lewisii

LINACEAE

The bright blue flowers of this slender-stemmed plant catch the eye, and were seen by Meriwether Lewis when he and Clark made the first transcontinental crossing of the wilderness which would become the United States of America. They noted in their journals that they passed through fields of blue, and wrote home about this flax which was so like the European variety.

Linum is an old name for flax. The common flax, *L. usitatissimum*, was brought over from home by the first settlers. The flax pic-tured here, named for Lewis, though easily grown, does not have as tough a fibre. It grows up to twenty inches high.

> 'Blue were her eyes as the Fairy Flax
> And her lips like the dawn at sea.'

So writes the poet Longfellow, in 'The Wreck of the Hesperus.' In these words we have a vivid description of the captain's daughter who was drowned in the storm which wrecked her father's ship.

Blooms from June to July on dry prairies and open sub-Alpine flats from Ontario to Alaska and south to California.

Yellow Goat's Beard, Salsify
Tragopogon pratensis
COMPOSITAE

Introduced to this continent by the early colonists, this dandelion-like plant has spread far and wide. It may be distinguished from the dandelion by its grasslike leaves that embrace the stem, its stronger, stiffer stem, by its greater height (from one to three feet), and by a slightly more open flower head. It also produces larger, more striking seed heads. The flowers always incline towards the sun and hence follow it in its course. They close about noontime so that it has long been known in England as Go-to-bed-at-noon. The flowers do not open on dark days. The generic name, *Tragopogon*, means goat's beard, while the specific name, *pratensis*, indicates that it grows in meadows and fields.

This and the purple-flowered species, called oyster-plant, were brought out from Europe for their edible roots and for their medicinal value. The Indians soon found this plant to their taste as food and also used it in the form of a chewing gum or candy made from the thickened juice, apparently as a relief from indigestion. The large, globular seed heads are often sprayed with a fixative and used in winter bouquets.

Blooms from May to October in fields, roadsides and waste places throughout a large part of southern Canada and the United States. The long-sepalled but very similar species, *T. major*, is more common in the west, right to the Pacific coast. Also in Eurasia.

Blue-eyed Grass
Sisyrinchium angustifolium

IRIDACEAE

Theophrastus, an early botanist, used the generic name for another plant and later it was transferred to this group, so the meaning is obscure. *Angustifolium* means narrow-leaved and indicates the grasslike leaves of most plants in this genus. This North American native has emigrated to Europe and grows widely in many places.

There are many other species of *Sisyrinchium*, some with white, pink, or yellow flowers as well as blue. This plant reaches a height of six to twenty-four inches. The flowers bloom for one day only, opening during the morning. They are fragile and die quickly if picked. It is best to leave them to produce their small, round seed capsules, and grow again another day.

Blooms from April to July in wet to dry meadows and thickets across Canada and throughout the United States.

Purple Milkvetch
Astragalus adsurgens (striatus)

LEGUMINOSAE

Astragalus is the Greek name for a legume, and *adsurgens* means rising straight upwards, as do the stems of this species. The leaves are finely hairy, and there are thirteen to twenty-five leaflets in each one.

This genus has many species in it, all difficult to identify. Some are very poisonous when eaten by cattle and sheep. This species is not listed as a dangerous one. In some others, the poison may be absorbed from the soil where selenium is present. Common on the open prairies, it is a beautiful sight as it grows in large clumps.

Blooms from June to August on the southern prairies of Canada and south into Colorado.

Blazing Star
Liatris cylindraceae

COMPOSITAE

As the name suggests, the blazing stars command attention, adding colourful accents to late summer and autumn fields. There are many species, resembling each other and frequently inter-breeding, which altogether cover a large part of the continent. Lavender and rose-purple are the normal colours though white forms also occur. This particular species is a slender member of the group, growing from eight inches to two feet high, having stiff, narrow, pointed leaves, with flowering heads that are loose, open and ragged. It is usually sparse but sometimes occurs in spectacular stands. Superficially like the knapweeds, it lacks the fringed floral bracts and branching character of those plants.

Some species of this native North American genus have been used in gardens and one wonders why more of these striking flowers have not been developed by the horticulturists.

This species blooms July to September in dry, open places, often sandy, from west New York and southern Ontario to Minnesota, south to Ohio and Arkansas.

Prickly Rose
Rosa acicularis

ROSACEAE

Almost all wild roses are pink or white flowers of shrubby habit, with or without thorns, and may be from one to eight feet high. They are regarded as weeds in agricultural areas, but they add beauty to roadsides, prairies, open woods and rocky places. Iowa, North Dakota, and Georgia chose wild roses as their state flowers. The provincial flower of Alberta is the prickly rose.

Roses were cultivated in remote times by Chinese, Japanese, Persian and Roman gardeners. In Roman times, the rose was the symbol of secrecy and when placed over an entrance to a meeting place, anyone entering bound himself not to reveal whatever transpired within. Hence the expression *sub rosa* which is still commonly used.

East of Sofia, Roumania, the Valley of Roses is one hundred miles long and twenty wide, and it is full of roses. From the petals of roses is pressed the oil known as attar of roses, a valuable component of perfumes. In pioneer days and more recently in England during the Second World War, rose hips were a valuable source of Vitamin C. Rose petals may be candied or used to make a delicately scented jelly.

Blooms from May to August on roadsides and open woods from Quebec to Alaska, and south to Colorado in the mountains.

Western Indian Paintbrush, Painted-cup
Castilleja miniata

SCROPHULARIACEAE

It is difficult to find a lovelier sight, in mid-summer, than an Alpine meadow red with paintbrush, set off by the blue of lupine and the white of bistort. This is the commonest of the more than two hundred species in the Americas.

On this plant, the true flowers are green, mostly covered by brilliant red bracts. The name paintbrush is appropriate, for these bracts look as if they had been dipped into red paint. The plants are semi-parasitic on the roots of other plants, but do not look like parasites, for they have green leaves and good root systems.

A Spanish botanist, Don Domingo Castilleja, is said to have been the first to find plants of this genus in Central America. The genus was named after him. *Miniata* is from minium, the scarlet-red oxide of lead. Occasionally, crimson or yellow-coloured bracts are found on plants of this species. The whole genus is very complex and the species are difficult to recognize. It grows to a height of one to two feet.

Blooms from June to September from Manitoba to British Columbia and south in mountain meadows.

Blueweed, Viper's Bugloss
Echium vulgare

BORAGINACEAE

Sweeps of blue in stony pastures or uncultivated fields in summer are likely to be blueweed—aesthetically charming or an obnoxious weed, depending upon your point of view. The pale to deep blue-purple flowers, with projecting red stamen, stud bristly stems, one to three feet tall, on short curling clusters that bear one open flower at a time. Pink or white blooms occasionally occur. The generic name, *Echium,* was used by the classical Greek, Dioscorides, because he thought the plant's nutlets resembled a viper's head.

Brought from Europe by both French and English colonists, probably because of its historic use in herbal remedies, it is now widely naturalized. Bees produce a supposedly medicinal blue honey from its nectar-rich blossoms, and the roots contain a deep red colouring matter. The name, viper's bugloss, reminds us that it was long regarded as a cure for snakebite in Europe.

Blooms from June to September (or to frost) in waste places, roadsides and dry, open fields from Nova Scotia to British Columbia, south to Georgia, Texas and Washington. Most common in Quebec, Ontario and the middle west. Also in Europe.

Woodlands

Whoever has entered a quiet leafless glade some early spring morning and has seen hepaticas flashing like forgotten jewels has ventured into the great deciduous forest of eastern North America. Maybe it was only a woodlot or perhaps a vale in a long reach of woods, but certainly it was one corner of that vast forest of maples, oaks and ashes and other deciduous trees that once reached unbroken from the Great Lakes to the Atlantic, and which still exists in patches and even long stretches despite all the development of the most settled part of this country.

Within its glens and glades, upon its slopes and in its valleys this forest enfolds a real treasury of flowers. Mostly these are spring flowers that prosper when warm sunlight reaches down through the yet unclothed branches of the trees. It is then that the hepaticas, the pink-faced spring beauties and the golden trout lilies display their delicate blooms. Then the forest floor is carpeted with white trillium, violets nod their purple, white or yellow heads, and wild ginger creeps almost unseen upon the leaf-strewn ground.

With the coming of the leaves this profusion of bloom will give way to shadow and mystery. Few flowers grow in the summer-darkened woods, yet those few will reward the seeker. In July will appear the graceful white umbels of the wild leeks, shy reminders of mats of green leaves that marked the spring woods and have now disappeared. Late in August the snowy blooms of the white snakeroot appear, and the gleam of the zigzag goldenrod and its cousin, the wreath goldenrod, adorn open woods and woodland paths. Some of these latter beauties will last until the enthralling glory of autumn comes to the deciduous forest, when the maples and their associated deciduous allies provide that breathtaking kaleidoscope of colour which is one of the marvels of the world.

As we move northward in the woods more and more evergreens begin to appear. They are scarce or completely lacking in the deciduous forest but farther north they become dominant. This in-between forest is thus a mixed forest that has characteristics of both the deciduous forest to the south and the conifer forest to the north. Its northern and southern bounds are blurred but it stretches from the Atlantic Ocean across the country far into the West.

In fact, paper birch, quaking aspen and balsam poplar carry their leafy banners to intermingle with the evergreens as far as British Columbia and the Yukon.

This forest too has its floral gems and among them are the waxy white, often pink-flushed blooms and polished green leaves of the trailing arbutus, so commonly associated with pines. Its spring luxuriance, happy reminder of the passing of winter, has caused the Nova Scotians to select it as their 'mayflower', their provincial emblem. Far at the other end of the forest another official floral emblem is to be found in the resplendent fireweed of the Yukon. What could be a more fitting symbol of sturdy survival than the great pink spires of fireweed springing up amidst the ashes of forest fires; a true Phoenix is this noble plant. Both of these plants, of course, grow from one end of the forest to the other.

Of all the forests of Canada the largest in extent is the northern conifer or boreal forest which covers approximately one-third of the country. Reaching from Newfoundland and the Maritimes in the east this vast forest crosses the Gaspé Peninsula, touches the shores of Lake Superior then sweeps up into the northern remoteness of the Prairie provinces, the Northwest Territories, the Yukon and Alaska. Nor does this forest in truth end there for it merges in Siberia with a boreal forest which is really circumpolar in extent. It sends long fingers down the continental mountains, both east and west, and down along the coasts where the climatic influence of cold waters favour its growth. In the north it extends to the tundra where its exploring forces are always thrusting forward into the open barren land.

Only a small number of plants are adapted to thrive in the cold, moist environment of this forest with its long, trying winters and mostly poorly-drained soils. So, it is dominated by a few evergreens. Of these white spruce and balsam fir are so common it is sometimes called the spruce-fir forest. In the wetter parts black spruce and that deciduous conifer, the tamarack, take over, while in drier areas the jack pine prospers. In general, then, here is a tremendous blanket of sombre green, relieved in part by birch, aspen and poplar.

In the dark depths of the boreal forest there are few

showy flowers. Yet he who has come upon some mossy knoll covered with the misty pink blooms of twinflower, or who has found that breathtaking beauty of the shaded dell, the calypso orchid, will scarcely feel any lack. It was calypso, one remembers, that made the great naturalist, John Muir, cry for joy when he first saw this beauty in Ontario. In the green shade of the forest the nodding white blooms of the one-flowered wintergreen stand out like forgotten snowflakes whilst the yellow delicacy of the naked mitrewort asks for discovery. Pink pyrolas march up exposed banks and in openings the jaunty bunchberry flaunts its white masses in summer and its polished red fruit in the fall. The dwarf blueberry, with its blue fruit and its flaming red mats of autumn foliage send unforgettable colour into the midst of endless green. No, floral beauty and colour are not lacking in this most extensive of all our woods.

Even the wide open prairies are not entirely without their woods. Wherever streams provide moisture and sheltering valleys, there one will be almost sure to find lines of cottonwoods and other poplars, willows, perhaps bur oak, box elder and other trees. Yet none of these is as noteworthy as the aspen with its dancing green summer leaves and its autumnal gold. To the settlers on the prairies, as to the Indians before them, the aspen was a valuable aid to living, providing poles for teepees, logs for cabins and wood that was burned in campfires and stoves.

There are few if any flowers that are peculiar to these scattered woodlands. But flowers there are, frequently in considerable abundance. It is, indeed, along the poplar bluffs and near the aspen groves that one commonly finds the lovely floral emblem of Alberta, the pink prickly rose, blooming at its best.

West of the prairies come the mountains, range after range for hundreds of miles, where everywhere ridge and peak rise through a cloak of green. This green is the widespread Cordilleran forest, which to the south is continental in extent and to the north marches to meet the boreal conifer forest with which it eventually merges. Like the boreal forest, the mountain woods are predominantly evergreen. Heavy and dark in part, especially to the north and on windward slopes, they are light with open glades and parkland in the south and on leeward slopes where dry conditions prevail. There are those, in fact, who would see the mountain forest as a southward extension of the great conifer forest of the north for when the trees of the north, reaching far south in cold valleys and on the heights, give way it is to similar evergreens. So closely related are these evergreens that some claim them to be simply varieties of the northern trees. Engelman spruce, it is said, is a variety of white spruce, Alpine fir a variety of balsam fir and lodgepole pine a variety of jack pine. Nonetheless, the observer must confess that, whatever the validity of this argument, there is a very different look and feel to the mountain forest from that of its boreal relation.

Anyone who has looked at the serried spires of Engelman spruce and lodgepole pine knows that these trees have a character all their own. Yet it is undoubtedly the mountain surroundings that make the most difference. Lodgepole pines often stand in massed ranks, black-green beside dashing mountain streams with the water frothing white beside them. Spruce and pine frequently stand close together on massively bulging ridges then cease altogether where tumbled grey talus slopes betoken the plunging cliffs that carry one's eyes up and up. Finally, there is an end to trees altogether at the tree line where so often the Alpine fir lives twisted, tortured and yet successful in the battle for existence. From the tree line our eyes may peer across the seeming emptiness of the treeless alpine meadow and tundra to the glistening purity of snowy peaks cutting their way into the blue sky beyond. Such vistas are everywhere in the mountains and so too is a variety of climatic and living conditions that give a varying form and character to the mountain forest that the monotonous boreal forest does not possess.

On a spring morning in this mountain woodland one can trudge a trail for miles through the silent trees until, all unprepared, one climbs over a last remaining snowdrift to find the sparkling waters of a pond, nestling beneath high cliffs and framed in white and gold. The white is snow, the gold is a border of glacier or avalanche lilies, growing in such profusion as to be countless to any viewer. Or one may drive along a mountain highway and come to a place where golden waves break down across the openings between the dark green groves of trees; again it is the glacier lily, a true herald of spring in these parts. No less a herald is the soft and silky, cream and grey-blue anemone that so often keeps company with the glacier lily in these same openings.

As the days pass by, calypso orchids (here commonly called fairy slippers) will appear in the lodgepole groves, singly, in groups, or sometimes by the hundreds. In the bushy openings of the dry woods of the southern mountains the wild clematis will set out blue stars to deck the green. Close by may be a glen where puffs of white smoke seem to be spouting up from the ground; as we approach them these puffs become fixed as the filmy white heads of that spectacular lily that carries the curious name of bear grass. When we climb some mountain trail and find beside it the glowing red jewel of the columbine, backed by the velvet black of the forest, we know that the short mountain summer has come. The smiling yellow faces of the balsam root may add an accent to this impression and even hint that summer must soon pass on. When that day comes the gold of flowers will give way to the gold of aspen leaves for this dancing tree dwells along with evergreens here as elsewhere. Throughout spring and summer in and around the mountain forest there is a wealth of bloom; then comes the brief resplendent fall and long winter's rest.

As one proceeds westward across the mountains each windward slope tends to receive more and more moisture from the prevailing westerly winds until the coast is reached. On the western slopes of the coastal range the ocean winds drop their heaviest loads — as much as 200 inches of rain a year in some parts of British Columbia. Thanks to the moderating influence of this oceanic climate there is combined with the wet a particularly long growing season. Hence it is in this moist, mild region that the great trees of the Pacific coast forest take over. Greatest of these is the Douglas fir. In good stands the trees average 200 feet in height, with the giants attaining 300 feet and more. The wealth of Douglas fir in this forest is witness to former fires or clearing, as this tremendous tree cannot reproduce itself in its own shade.

Without the aid of fire and clearing it must eventually give way to those other great trees, the western cedar and western hemlock. In the older climax sections of the coastal forest these trees predominate. Along the shoreline, where salt spray rains upon the land, another huge tree, the Sitka spruce, holds sway. Again we are dealing with an evergreen forest where there are only a few deciduous trees. Only one of these, the broad-leaved maple, reaches any size in a woodland where size is an outstanding characteristic.

Continually bathed by Pacific rains that provide the moisture upon which it depends, this forest would probably, if left to itself, become in large part a rain forest. In some of its oldest and least disturbed sections this development may be seen, best of all, perhaps, at Cathedral Grove on Vancouver Island. There, high overhead, the soaring trees arch like the groins of a cathedral vault. Through all the wood a profound quiet prevails in the midst of a luminescent gloom that is shot through with a dim green light filtering down from the forest roof far above. Moisture is everywhere, sustaining the thick mosses that cushion every footstep. Within this cathedral of nature the visitor can only stand in wonder and awe.

In the wet Pacific forest, the woodland of the tall trees, mosses, ferns and epiphytes flourish. Flowering plants find it less attractive than the moisture-loving, shade-enduring ferns and mosses. Even so there are flowers. Some are almost unbelievable curiosities, like the red and white candystick, so much like a Christmas candy cane, or the branching pinesap, which makes one think of a cluster of small, inverted pipes. Some are of exquisite beauty, like the striped coralroot which, seen with the sunlight shining behind it, glistens like purest crystal. The queen cup and the large white trillium dot the spring woods with their snowy blooms. The vanilla leaf dusts the air with its tiny white flowers and spreads out its deeply cleft green leaves. These leaves when dry have a sweet aroma that earns for this interesting plant a second name, sweet-after-death. To the people of British Columbia the most attractive flower of the coastal woods is their provincial flower, the Pacific dogwood, whose creamy blooms cascade along the banks of streams.

Wild Ginger
Asarum canadense

ARISTOLOCHIACEAE

The leaves of wild ginger usually grow so close together that the small red-brown flowers are hidden. The plant grows from a branching rhizome and likes moist shady slopes in rich deciduous woods. The root, when cleaned and peeled, was used by several Indian tribes as a flavouring. Though unrelated to true ginger, the root has a distinctly ginger taste. Pioneer women cooked it with sugar to use as a spice.

The ground-level flowers are pollinated by crawling insects. The leaves may reach a height of six to twelve inches. On the Pacific coast another species, *A. caudatum* is similar but has long trailing tips to its petals.

Blooms in April and May from Quebec to Manitoba, south to Alabama and west to Kansas.

Fringed Polygala, Gaywings
Polygala paucifolia
POLYGALACEAE

Like butterflies with their wings arched or spread the showy rose-purple flowers of fringed polygala lie among thick, dark-green leaves. The 'wings' are two of the sepals that are petal-like, while the three petals are bound together in a keel or tube which terminates in a fringed crest. When a bee lands on this crest the pistil and stamens are forced up out of a slit in the top of the keel and so come into contact with the pollen-laden bee, thus assuring cross-fertilization. Occasionally a whole group of these flowers will be white.

Blooms from May to July in rich, damp woods from New Brunswick and Quebec to Manitoba, south to Connecticut, Illinois and Minnesota; in the mountains to Georgia and Tennessee.

Rosy Twisted Stalk, Mandarin
Streptopus roseus

LILIACEAE

Hardly noticeable in the dim woods are the tiny pink nodding flowers held beneath the leaves of the rosy twisted stalk. The generic name is literally translated to give the common name, both of which refer to the twisted flower stems of some species. The cherry-red berries that develop in late summer do not long remain attached to the stems, probably because they fall off so easily. These berries are said to be laxative and were called scoot berries by country folk.

The height of the plant is up to three feet. A similar species, *S. amplexifolius*, has greenish-white flowers. This one is circumboreal and is found in northern Europe and Asia.

Blooms from April to July in rich woods from Newfoundland and Labrador to Alaska, south to Oregon, Minnesota and Georgia.

Indian Cucumber-root
Medeola virginiana

LILIACEAE

This delicate member of the lily family, like several of its larger relatives, has recurved petals and sepals. In an interesting colour combination their pale yellow provides a nice setting for the reddish-brown, spreading stamens. The flowers, in a loose umbel at the top of a plant (that may rise from eight inches to three feet), face downward, dangling underneath a whorl of three leaves and above a second whorl of five to nine leaves. In late summer red-purple berries stand up above the now purple-tinged leaves.

This genus is named *Medeola* after the ancient sorceress, Medea, because of its supposed medicinal values. The specific name, *virginiana,* refers to Virginia from which the first known specimens were taken to Europe. The common name refers to the crisp, white rhizome or underground stem, which tastes like cucumber and has been used as food, either fresh in salads, or pickled and roasted.

Blooms in May and June in rich woods and on mossy banks from Quebec to Minnesota, south to Florida and Louisiana.

Queen Cup
Clintonia uniflora

LILIACEAE

One of the two western species of this genus, queen cup enjoys damp coniferous woods, especially in the mountains. It blooms with a single white flower on a stem three to six inches tall. This flower is succeeded by a single blue beadlike fruit.

The generic name, *Clintonia,* was first given to the eastern yellow-flowered plant by the botanist, Asa Gray, in honour of De Witt Clinton, naturalist and governor of New York State. There are six species, two in the east, two in the west and two in Asia.

The English name does not seem appropriate, as the flower is more flat than cup-shaped in full bloom. Though it has six petals, their pure white shines out in the dark coniferous woods like stars. Star lily might be more suggestive, and it is now well known that stars are really not five-pointed.

Blooms from May to August in the higher areas of the Rockies and Coastal ranges, Alaska to Alberta and south to California.

Calypso, Fairy Slipper
Calypso bulbosa

ORCHIDACEAE

Hiding in the dark places of the forests where it is always cool, small calypso deserves its name, the Greek word for concealment. Homer writes of the lovely nymph Calypso, daughter of Atlas, who lived in a cavern sheltered by thickets and grapevines on the island of Ogypia. She welcomed the shipwrecked Odysseus and persuaded him to stay with her for seven years. The flower named after this lovely goddess is probably the most alluring of all our native orchids, and has fascinated all who know it.

There are two forms, one occurring from the Rockies eastward with a yellow beard on the slipper lip, the other, with a white beard, on the Pacific coast. The petals and sepals, which are similar, are erect and spreading above the lip. They vary in colour from pale to deep magenta, except in the rare white form. The lip is shaped like a tiny flaring slipper, white marked with magenta. The reddish stem is three to eight inches in height. One basal leaf and the single flower grow from a tiny corm, which is only lightly attached to moss or soil and easily uprooted. Snails and slugs and thoughtless people destroy these delicate plants, and in time they will probably disappear altogether, if not protected.

Blooms from May to July in mossy calcareous woods from Newfoundland and Labrador to Alaska, and south to the mountains of Arizona and California.

Painted Trillium
Trillium undulatum

LILIACAEA

The species name *undulatum* means wavy, and describes the edges of the petals. Like other trilliums, all parts are in threes. The lovely red markings at the base of each petal distinguish this trillium from all others and makes the common name very appropriate. This flower is smaller and later blooming than the great white trillium, and grows to a height of eight to twelve inches.

Blooms in May and June in the cool northern woods from New Brunswick to Manitoba and Wisconsin, and south in the uplands to Tennessee and Georgia.

Large-flowered Bellwort
Uvularia grandiflora

LILIACEAE

The flowers of the bellwort hang like golden lamps in the growing shade of the springtime woods. Ornamented with gracefully twisted petals and sepals, this lily, with flowers up to two inches long, rises up through the rich green background of a broad leaf through which it seems to pierce, the whole plant growing from six to thirty inches above the ground. It is similar to the perfoliate bellwort, which has smaller flowers, its floral parts being roughened inside by glands and its leaves whitened underneath. The large-flowered bellwort, on the other hand, has its petals and sepals smooth inside and its leaves downy underneath, not whitened. The generic name, *Uvularia*, means hanging like a uvula or palate.

This was one of the first North American plants to attract the attention of European explorers and is described in a book on Canadian plants as early as 1635. It was used by the Indians in various medicinal preparations and has been cultivated with some success in woodland gardens.

Blooms from April to June in rich deciduous woods, chiefly calcareous, from Quebec to North Dakota, south to Georgia and Oklahoma.

Showy Orchis
Orchis spectabilis

ORCHIDACEAE

Once a common orchid of rich woods, this species is becoming increasingly hard to find. The flower stem, rising from between two large basal leaves, grows to a height of four to twelve inches. The soft colours of mauve and white seem to belong on the shady slope of its favourite haunts, where Christmas fern uncurls its graceful fronds. The English name is a direct translation of the Latin, but is not very appropriate. It is a beautiful plant, but not showy.

Two species of orchis live in continental North America, another in Asia. In northern regions, *Orchis rotundifolia* is abundant, its habitat extending from Labrador to Alaska and south in a few northern States. *Orchis spectabilis* is more common in the southeast.

Blooms from May to July from New Brunswick to Minnesota and south to Kansas and Alabama.

Devil's Club
Oplopanax horridum

ARALIACEAE

The very large leaves (up to twelve inches wide), and the thick stems (four to ten feet high) all bristling with spines, should be easily recognized and avoided if possible. Punctures made with these long spines are poisoned and can become swollen and very painful. Its English name is most appropriate. The generic name is from the two Greek words, *hoplon,* meaning weapon, and *panax,* the name of another large-leaved member of this family. *Horridum* is easy to understand once you have seen the innumerable spines on leaves and stems. The plant has small greenish-white flowers, which are followed by handsome scarlet berries. Dr. Cheadle, who crossed the continent from east to west in 1862–63, writes in his journal of the 'infernally prickly trailing plant whose spines pierced our moccasins and clothes, and tripped our horses.' However, if regarded from a safe distance, the large maple-shaped leaves and brilliant red fruit are truly beautiful.

Blooms in June (fruit: July and August) from western Ontario to British Columbia, north to Alaska and south to California.

154

Moccasin Flower, Stemless Lady's Slipper, Pink Lady's Slipper
Cypripedium acaule

ORCHIDACEAE

Growing in partial shade in acid woods and bogs, the pink moccasin flower is called stemless because there is no other stem than the flower stalk which rises to a height of fifteen inches. The colour of pink varies from pale to very deep. White flowers are not uncommon, especially in more northerly regions.

Pollination is effected only by large insects, such as bumblebees, which are capable of forcing an entrance into the 'slipper' by pushing apart the halves of the pouch, probably at the top centre of the slit where the white markings may act as insect guides. The design of the slipper is called an insect ambush because, once inside the smooth steep walls make climbing out impossible. However, there is a hairy path in the centre that leads to the sticky stigma where previously collected pollen is left. Then one of two exits may be used, causing the insect to squeeze past the anthers collecting pollen on the way out.

Orchid seeds are extremely small and produced in great quantity. It is said to take twelve to fifteen years for the seeds of most of our lady's slippers to grow to a flowering plant. Like all orchids they require special conditions in which to develop and do not thrive in most gardens. Picking the flowers not only reduces the number of seeds, but sometimes destroys the plant.

Blooms from April to July from Newfoundland to Alberta and south to Georgia and Alabama.

Pacific Dogwood, Western Dogwood
Cornus nuttallii

CORNACEAE

Early spring brings the Pacific dogwood into bloom when its pure white petal-like bracts unfold and reveal the green flower buds. These large bracts are pointed in this species and vary in number from four to six or seven. In the centre the tiny flowers are greenish-white when they open. This plant is a tree which may grow up to sixty feet in height under favourable conditions. The average height is about thirty feet. It is a favourite tree to plant in gardens on the west coast. In early autumn, a compact cluster of bright red berries takes the place of the flowers.

Named for Thomas Nuttall (1786–1859), who was one of the first botanical explorers of western North America, it is the official emblem of British Columbia, and is protected by law in that province. The generic name is from the Latin *cornu,* a horn. This alludes to the hardness of the wood, which has long been used for skewers. Dogwood comes from 'Dagwood,' derived from the old English *dagge,* a dagger or sharp-pointed object.

Blooms from April to June from British Columbia south to California.

Blue Cohosh
Caulophyllum thalictroides

BERBERIDACEAE

In the bare woods of early spring the smooth, purple-grey stems and unfolding leaf of the blue cohosh catch the eye. The small, greenish-yellow flowers are, however, unobtrusive and are noticeable only when the mature stamens dot them with yellow. The large, compound leaf later expands, turns green and looks like meadow rue. The whole plant reaches up from two to four feet tall. In the summer the berry-like fruit turns a brilliant blue.

The generic name, *Caulophyllum,* means stem-leaf, and indicates that the stem seems to form a stalk for the very large leaf. The specific name, *thalictroides,* means that the leaves resemble those of meadow rue which is called *Thalictrum.* It is sometimes called papoose root because the Indians believed concoctions made from it helped in childbirth. It has been used in folk medicine in various ways and its seeds have been made a substitute for coffee.

Blooms from April to June in rich, moist woods from New Brunswick to Manitoba, south to South Carolina, Alabama and Missouri. Also eastern Asia.

Yellow Lady's Slipper
Cypripedium calceolus

ORCHIDACEAE

The grace and beauty of most species in this genus are exemplified in this plant. There are several varieties, each of which used to be classified as a separate species. The size of the flower, colour and length of the two twisted petals, the hairiness and the height of the plant were until recently all used as distinguishing characters. Like some other cypripediums, the hairy variety *pubescens* may cause dermatitis when handled by some people. It is reported that the dried and ground-up root was used by the Indians as a sleeping potion.

Cypripedium is derived from two Greek words meaning the shoe of Aphrodite, and *calceolus* means little shoe. It reaches a height of eight to twenty-eight inches. The flower pictured is probably *C. calceolus var. planipetalum*.

When its habitat is being destroyed by highway building or farming, this orchid can be transplanted to a moist shady garden with some hope of success. It is the most easily grown of all the wild lady's slippers, though it must be protected from cutworms, slugs and too much heat.

Blooms from April to August throughout Canada and the northern United States in bogs and rich woodlands; also occasionally in Europe and Asia.

Orange Honeysuckle
Lonicera ciliosa
CAPRIFOLIACEAE

Named for Adam Lonitzer (1528–1586), an early German botanist, this genus has many species of vines in it. The very showy flowers, which may be pale or deep orange-red, are clustered within the paired terminal leaves which are joined at their bases. *Ciliosa* means fringed or hairy, referring to the marginal hairs of these leaves. The vine twines over bushes and trees up to twenty feet high. It is a favourite flower with hummingbirds.

Blooms in May and June in British Columbia and Montana, and south to California.

Bloodroot
Sanguinaria canadensis

PAPAVERACEAE

Coming up through the soft soil and dead leaves of early spring, the buds are enfolded in the large leaves to protect them from the cold. Whenever the sun shines and warms them, the flowers of the bloodroot open, but their pure white petals soon fall. The plant grows to a height of six to twelve inches.

The generic name is from the Latin word *sanguis*, meaning blood, and refers to the red juice of the plant, which is most copious in the root. The plant was valuable to both Indians and pioneers as a dye for clothing and baskets, and as face paint. They called it puccoon.

Blooms from March to May in rich open woods from Quebec to Manitoba and south to Florida.

Red Flowering Currant
Ribes sanguineum

GROSSULARIACEAE

One of the most beautiful flowering shrubs on the west coast, this currant grows in open woods and along roadsides. It varies in colour from pink to deep red, growing from four to eight feet high. The colour of its flowers and their sweet nectar attract the hummingbirds, of which there are several species on the west coast. Its dark currants are hardly edible and have a poor flavour.

Both Archibald Menzies and David Douglas reported this lovely shrub. Douglas took seeds back to England in 1827, and sold them, making enough money, it is reported, to pay for his two-year expedition. It has long been a favourite in gardens on the west coast and in England.

Blooms from March to May, west of the Cascades, from southern British Columbia south to northern California.

Dutchman's Breeches
Dicentra cucullaria

FUMARIACEAE

Every breeze sways the slender flower stalk of
this fragile plant which may be found in cool
shady woods in spring. The English name
comes from a fanciful resemblance to old-
fashioned Dutchman's breeches as they might
be seen hung on a line to dry. The generic
name is from the Greek, *dis,* meaning twice,
and *kentron,* a spur. This describes the two
inflated spurs of the flower which hold nectar
deep within. Since only a long-tongued insect
can reach the nectar via the opening at the
bottom, one can often see the hole bitten into
the top of the spur by short-tongued bees to
steal the nectar, thus bypassing pistil and
stamens. This action does not achieve pollination.

The plant grows to a height of five to nine
inches. The picture is of the pink form, with
orange accents, instead of the commoner
white with yellow.

Blooms from April to June from southeast
Canada west to North Dakota and south in
the mountains to Georgia.

Wild Blue Phlox
Phlox divaricata

POLEMONIACEAE

In May the open woodlands are filled with great colonies of the wild blue phlox. The plant grows from one or two feet tall, with spreading heads of pale pink to blue-purple and red-purple (occasionally white) blooms up to several inches across. Its paired, sharp-pointed leaves, hairy and sticky stems, along with the commonly notched petals, help to identify this phlox. It has close relatives in the south and midwest.

The generic name, *Phlox*, is on old Greek word meaning flame. Once applied to another genus, it is now reserved for this basically North American genus. The specific name, *divaricata*, means strongly divergent and describes the branching of the inflorescence. Long a favourite plant in gardens on this continent, many forms and hybrids have been developed by horticulturists from the original wild stock.

Its 'blue' is a perennial challenge to photographers, who find it fascinating but extremely difficult to reproduce because of the red element's tendency to come out predominant. The flower is rarely if ever a true blue in spite of the common name, though the mass effect is likely to be blueish.

Flowers from April to June in open, often rocky woods and fields from Quebec and Ontario to Minnesota and Nebraska, south to Florida and Texas.

Wild Geranium
Geranium maculatum

GERANIACEAE

All species of wild geranium develop a long pointed seed pod which resembles the bill of a crane. The generic name is from the Greek *geranos,* meaning crane. *Maculatum* means spotted, and possibly refers to the darker veins of the petals.

The Indians used the young leaves as a vegetable. Since all parts of the plant contain tannin, a tea was brewed from it to treat dysentery. It grows readily from seeds, and adapts to gardens easily. The seed pods when ripe, split suddenly and throw the seeds around. Its mauve flowers are attractive in spring, reaching a height of eighteen inches. In fall the leaves turn red.

Blooms from May to July, from Manitoba and Maine and south to Georgia and Kansas.

Indian Pipe
Monotropa uniflora
MONOTROPACEAE

Eerily white in the darkness of the summer woods, these curious plants seem like little pipes stuck in the ground by ghostly hands. Their whiteness, occasionally flushed with pink, indicates that they are saprophytic and parasitic in habit, living on the humus litter of the forest floor and even enlisting the aid of fungi in doing so. Growing from two inches to a foot high, often in dense clumps, the flowers point downward in bloom but turn upright, becoming dark brown and woody in texture when the fruit is ripe. In this latter state they may be seen throughout the winter, standing out against the snow.

The generic name, *Monotropa*, means turned to one side and describes the position of the top of the flowering stem. This is a very ancient plant, being a relic of the Tertiary Age. It has been utilized in folk medicine for the treatment of nervous troubles and for sore eyes.

Blooms from June to September in woodland humus. especially favouring coniferous forests, across Canada and the United States, south to Mexico; also in eastern Asia.

Virginia Cowslip,
Virginia Bluebell
Mertensia virginica

BORAGINACEAE

Favouring the flood plain of rivers as its habitat and extending into rich woods, this bluebell is not related to the bluebell, *Campanula rotundifolia,* illustrated elsewhere in this book. The buds are pink, but the mature flowers are usually sky blue, and often grow in such profusion as to create a blue woodland scene.

It grows well in gardens, though its deep root makes it almost impossible to transplant. Seeds are usually plentiful, grow readily and produce flowers in about three years. It is wise to plant the seeds where they will be undisturbed, as the leaves die down after blooming time, or about that time if no seeds are produced, and the plant may be destroyed by digging too close.

The generic name honours Franz Karl Mertens (1764–1831), a German botanist. In full bloom, it is eight to twenty-four inches high. Several other species are known in North America—*M. paniculata, M. longiflora* in the west, and *M. maritima* on the Atlantic shores and across the north from Greenland to Alaska.

Blooms from March to May or June in southern Ontario and New York, and south to Virginia, the Carolinas and west to Kansas.

Naked Mitrewort, Bishop's Cap
Mitella nuda

SAXIFRAGACEAE

This fragile beauty is a challenge to find in its preferred habitats. Although it is not rare, its green delicacy easily merges with its surroundings and causes it to be readily overlooked. It is a prize well worth the search, however, for once the searcher has seen its lacy, green-gold petals under a good magnifying glass he will never forget their charm.

This species ordinarily has no leaf on the stem, hence the name 'naked.' Its better-known relative, the two-leaved bishop's cap —a white-flowered dweller in open, rocky woods—has, as its name implies, a pair of leaves well up the stem. The naked species grows from one to eight inches high and its larger relative from four to eighteen inches. In both plants the fruit is shaped like a mitre, hence the common names.

Blooms from May to August in cool bogs, swamps and damp woods from Labrador to Mackenzie, south to Pennsylvania, Michigan, North Dakota and Montana; also in Asia. Two-leaved bishop's cap (*M. diphylla*) blooms from April to June in rich, often rocky woods from Quebec and Ontario to Minnesota, south to Virginia, Alabama and Missouri.

Partridge Berry
Mitchella repens

RUBIACEAE

Snaking along the woodland floor, the blue-green roundish leaves, patterned often with white lines, are usually the first sign of the partridge berry. Two by two, they march along the stems which in spring bear twinned flowers at their ends. These tube-like, fragile blooms are hairy and white inside, pinkish and smooth outside. One red berry arises from each pair of fertilized flowers and these berries, conspicuous among the evergreen leaves, stay on all winter.

The generic name, *Mitchella,* commemo-rates Dr. John Mitchell, a resident of colonial Virginia and a correspondent of Linnaeus in the eighteenth century. The specific name, *repens,* means creeping. As the common name suggests, the berries are favoured by the partridge or ruffed grouse, and also by bobwhite, wild turkeys, foxes, skunks and white-footed mice. The Indians were accustomed to eat these berries and used them medicinally. This plant is grown often in terraria.

Blooms from May to June in dry or moist woods from Newfoundland to Minnesota, south to Florida and Texas.

Pink Rhododendron
Rhododendron macrophyllum

ERICACEAE

One of the loveliest sights in early summer is a fine group of these shrubs. The large pink blooms, with a centre of almost red buds, are quite magnificent along the highway leading into Manning Park, in British Columbia. These shrubs frequently grow to ten feet in height, with bunches of flowers six inches across. It is the state flower of Washington and is protected by law in British Columbia. In spite of this, it is becoming increasingly rare, and should be treasured wherever it grows.

Macrophyllum means large-leaved. In this species the leaves may be six inches long, and grow in whorls setting off the large flower clusters. Few, if any, other species of this genus in North America are more beautiful in flower. These plants are toxic to livestock, mostly to sheep. The generic name is derived from the Greek words, *rhodon,* a rose, and *dendron,* a tree.

Blooms late May to early July in moist woods in western British Columbia and south to California.

One-flowered Wintergreen, Single Delight
Moneses uniflora

PYROLACEAE

In the mysterious green-filtered light of some damp wood in the north, perhaps under white cedars or tamarack, one is likely to come upon the delicate, creamy-white beauty of the one-flowered wintergreen. Held three to six inches above the ground, its white bloom seems like a large snowflake suspended in air, overarching a green ball (the ovary) and an exquisitely sculptured spike (the pistil). It rises above shiny green basal leaves which resemble those of pipsissewa and pyrola, its close relatives.

The name, *Moneses,* means single delight, referring to the fact that each plant has a single flower. It is of interest that this is also a monotypic genus, a one-of-a-kind beauty. Hard to find, the discovery of this gem provides a stellar moment in any seeker's day.

Blooms from June to August in cool, mossy woods and bogs from Greenland to Alaska, south to Pennsylvania, Michigan, Minnesota, New Mexico and Oregon. Around the world in the north (Eurasia).

Trailing Arbutus, Mayflower
Epigaea repens

ERICACEAE

The appearance of dainty, shell-pink or white blossoms resting among mats of thick, rounded leaves beside relict snowdrifts, herald the advent of the trailing arbutus in the spring. Where it is massed a haunting, spicy fragrance may pervade the air. Though widespread, this little shrub, six to twelve inches long, is rather choosy about where it grows and will usually be found in the neighbourhood of evergreen woods.

The generic name, *Epigaea,* means on the earth, and this is strengthened by the specific name, *repens,* that signifies creeping, both descriptive of the plant's habits.

The delightful arbutus has been chosen as the provincial flower of Nova Scotia, where it is called mayflower. Yet its charm has led in many areas to overpicking and extermination, so that it is widely protected by law in many states and needs even further protection. The Pilgrim Fathers, it is said, had a particular affection for this plant whose springtime blooms assured them that their first gruelling winter was over.

Blooms from March to May in sandy or peaty woodlands, preferring acid soils, from Labrador and Newfoundland to Saskatchewan and south to Florida, Mississippi and Iowa.

Twin-flower
Linnaea borealis

CAPRIFOLIACEAE

In dark northern woods no sight is more
entrancing than the pink twin-flowers,
marching two by two along their creeping
evergreen stems across some ancient moss-
covered log or filling some sunlit glade with
companies so vast as to perfume the air.
Rising only two to four inches above the
ground, these delicate pink bells may yet
seem massive in their profusion. They are,
indeed, one of the most familiar plants of the
northern wilds, and this is true of most of the
northern world as they are circumpolar in
extent.

It is little wonder that this was the favourite flower of Linnaeus, the father of modern
botany, who loved it in the forests of his
native Sweden and who delighted in having
his portrait painted while holding a sprig of
this flower. So it was fitting that in 1737 the
twin-flower should have been named *Linnaea*
in his honour by his friend Gronovius.

Blooms from June to August, occasionally
in the autumn, in cool woods, especially
coniferous forests, bogs and peaty places
from Greenland to Alaska and south to
Maryland, West Virginia, Indiana, South
Dakota, Utah and northern California; also
Eurasia.

Broad-leaved Spring Beauty
Claytonia caroliniana

PORTULACACEAE

The tiny bulbs of this plant were used by Indians and early settlers as a spring food. Boiled in salted water, they are said to taste like chestnuts. However, one would need to find a great many and dig deeply for each pea-sized bulb to get enough to eat. Squirrels, chipmunks and even bears are said to enjoy them.

The plant is named after John Clayton, an early American botanist, who made plant collections in the 1700s. The single, weak stem, three to twelve inches high, bears two opposite leaves and several flowers. The five pink-veined, pink or white petals of each flower fade as they age. Though described as scentless by some botanists, a lovely fragrance pervades the air where there are many flowers. There are several species of *Claytonia* across North America.

Blooms from March to July in rich woods from Newfoundland to Saskatchewan, west to Minnesota and south in the mountains to North Carolina and Tennesee.

Purple Fringed Orchid
Habenaria psycodes

ORCHIDACEAE

In midsummer, mounds of purple which appear along the banks of woodland streams, by the open edges of cedar bogs and out in the swamp should be examined with care, for this is the manner of growth of the purple fringed orchid. Its many-flowered racemes of lilac or rose-purple blooms, each one butterfly-like in shape with a delicately fringed lip, top plants that may be from eight inches to three feet tall. In some cases the flowering racemes themselves can be eight inches or more high. A large form occurs which has hitherto been called a separate species (*H. fimbriata*) but recent studies show a regular intergradation between the two so that they are now regarded as varieties of the same species.

The generic name, *Habenaria,* means throng or rein, and refers to the shape of the lip of some of the species in this genus. The specific name, *psycodes,* means like a butterfly. Thoreau called this beauty the 'belle of the swamp,' and certainly it is one of the loveliest of our summer flowers.

Blooms from June to August in wet, open woods, swamps, bogs, roadside ditches, etc., especially where acid soil exists, from Newfoundland to Ontario and Minnesota, south to New Jersey, Indiana and Arkansas; in the mountains to Georgia and Tennessee.

Arrowleaf Balsamroot
Balsamorhiza sagittata

COMPOSITAE

Discovered by Lewis and Clark, this is the most common species of this genus. It grows to a height of from ten to thirty inches in prairie grassland, and on open hillsides.

The great leaves, shaped like arrowheads, are indicated in the first part of the common name. The second part and the generic name come from the Greek words for balsam and root. When the rind of the woody taproot is pealed off, the heart is edible, and was used as food by both Indians and pioneers. The seeds were ground to make pinole — the name for a biscuit made from this special 'flour.' The young green shoots were boiled as a vegetable. At one time, these roots were sent to France, where they were used as food and called 'pommes de Canada'.

Blooms from April to July in Alberta and British Columbia and south to Colorado and California.

Wintergreen, Checkerberry
Gaultheria procumbens

ERICACEAE

The plump red berries of the wintergreen, enticingly attractive amidst their shiny, evergreen leaves, are eagerly sought. The berries are refreshing and tasty, while the aromatic leaves, when young and tender, have frequently been used as a substitute for tea, notably in the American Revolutionary War when, after the Boston Tea Party, the New Englanders were short of tea. This plant is the original source of oil of wintergreen and is still occasionally used for that purpose; however, most of the oil now comes from black birch which gives the same flavour.

The urn-shaped, waxy white flowers, similar to those of the blueberry, nestle in the axils of the leaves in midsummer, a little above the ground, and are far less conspicuous than the berries.

Specimens of this plant were sent by Dr. Gaulthier of Quebec to Linnaeus through Peter Kalm in the mid-eighteenth century. Hence the genus was named *Gaultheria* for him, though it had reached France as early as the end of the sixteenth century, sent by Dr. Sarrasin, and was noted in a book published there in 1700.

Blooms in July and August in open woods on acid soil, commonly among conifers, from Newfoundland to Manitoba and south to Georgia and Alabama.

Cut-leaved Toothwort
Dentaria laciniata

CRUCIFERAE

This is the commonest of the toothworts that decorate the eastern deciduous woods in early spring. Its whorl of three leaves, well up the eight- to fifteen-inch stem, each divided into three to five narrow, deeply-toothed segments, identifies it from its relative, the broad-leaved toothwort or crinkleroot which has two leaves with broad segments, slightly toothed. The quarter- to half-inch flowers have four petals like other members of the mustard family and are white or pale lavender. It often forms large colonies.

The rhizomes, or underground stems, are white, crisp and tasty, with a flavour much like that of watercress; hence, they have been popular as a salad ingredient or condiment.

Blooms from March to June in rich, moist woods, especially on calcareous soils, from Quebec to Minnesota and Nebraska, south to Florida, Louisiana and Kansas.

Hepatica
Hepatica acutiloba

RANUNCULACEAE

Among the matted brown leaves of last year, only recently rid of winter's snow, we shall find the fuzzy, grey buds and the colourful blooms of the hepatica, herald of spring in the deciduous woods. Rising just above the ground and looking like small anemones, to which they are closely related, they range in colour from white through pink to blue and purple. The new, three-lobed leaves appear only after the flowers have bloomed, though the old leaves, usually flattened upon the ground, are still attached to the plant.

The name *Hepatica,* meaning pertaining to the liver, refers to the supposed likeness of the leaf to the shape of the human liver. Because of this fancied resemblance, it was thought in medieval times the hepatica plants were a major remedy for liver troubles. The Indians also used the plant as a medicine and as a charm on traps set for fur-bearing animals.

Two closely similar species, *H. acutiloba,* the pointed-leaves species, illustrated here, and *H. americana,* the round-leaved species, bloom at the same time, March to June. The first ranges from Quebec to Minnesota, south to Georgia, Alabama and Missouri; the second from Nova Scotia to Manitoba, south to Florida and Missouri.

Common Blue Violet
Viola papilionacea

VIOLACEAE

One of the most familiar violets, this is found in damp woods and meadows, and grows in a variety of heights up to eight inches. *Viola* was the Latin name used for these flowers at the time of Virgil, and *papilionacea* means 'like a butterfly.' Violets were believed to be powerful against evil spirits and a compress of violets was a popular remedy for headaches. The flowers are edible and high in Vitamin C. Violet flowers can be coated with sugar, used as a candy or as an ornament for other foods.

Blue to purple violets have been favourites for thousands of years. They grow throughout the world on every continent, and there are at least forty species of blue violets in North America. Four states—Illinois, New Jersey, Rhode Island and Wisconsin—and the province of New Brunswick have chosen a blue violet as their emblem. Violets were the Emperor Napoleon's favourite flowers and became the emblem of his followers.

Violets have cleistogamic, or blind, flowers which develop without coloured petals; they look like green buds and never open until the seeds are developed. These green buds are self-fertilizing and help to ensure seeds for reproduction.

Blooms from March to June from New Brunswick to Manitoba, throughout the eastern United States and west to Oklahoma.

Pink Erythronium
Pink Easter Lily, Red Lily
Erythronium revolutum

LILIACEAE

Like many of its relatives, this lily blooms in spring. Its three petals and three sepals are alike and pure pink. They curve backwards, revealing the six bright yellow stamens and the pistil. The two large basal leaves are dark green marked with light green. Its name is taken from the Greek word for red, *erythros,* and the Latin, *revolutum,* referring to the recurved petals and sepals. The flowers grow to a height of six to twelve inches, one to each stem. The plants need protection and should not be transplanted, as they require the special habitat of a sandy flood plain, and a mild climate.

There are fifteen species of this genus, one in Europe, two in eastern North America, and all the others in the west. The European species, *E. dens-canis,* is the only other pink one.

Blooms from March to May in the river valleys of Vancouver Island, and in Washington and Oregon on the Pacific slopes.

Pipsissewa
Chimaphila umbellata

PYROLACEAE

The whorls of thick, dark green, shiny leaves that embellish this plant are often the first thing to attract attention upon some woodland slope. Then at the top of a stem, four to twelve inches high, may be seen the inch-wide, waxy flowers—pink or cream-coloured, noticeably green-centred, and gathered in loose umbels above the leaves.

The generic name, *Chimaphila,* means winter lover, and refers to the evergreen character of the plant. The common name is a modified Indian term and it reminds us that the Indians used pipsissewa both as a tea and as a medicine. In popular medicine generally it has been widely used. Its leaves, which many people like to chew, are used in making root beer.

Blooms from June to August in dry woods, particularly evergreen forest, from Quebec to Alaska and south to Georgia, Ohio, Illinois, Utah and California; also Eurasia.

Great White Trillium
Trillium grandiflorum

LILIACEAE

A true native of North America, this is the largest species of trillium which blooms in spring in rich woodlands of North America. The large white flower usually has all parts in threes as the genus name suggests. As the flower ages, it turns pink, sometimes becoming a deep magenta. The flower and the plant are both extremely variable. Petals may be white, or white streaked with green, or all green. They can increase in numbers to four, six or more. Stamens may be lacking, especially in the double forms. Number of leaves is also variable.

There are about twenty-eight species of this genus in North America. They range from white to pink, red, purple and yellow. They are all bulbous plants. Unfortunately many people pick them each spring, and because the leaves are all picked with the flower, the bulb dies. Thus the beauty of our woods disappears, as picking destroys the plant. *Trillium grandiflorum* is the provincial flower of Ontario.

Blooms from March to May from Quebec south to Georgia, and west to Minnesota.

Index of flowers
by common name

Index of flowers
by botanical name

Index of flowers
by family

Photographers